Learn to
SEW
with Lauren

Learn to SEW with Lauren

From first stitches to
personalized projects

Lauren Guthrie

MITCHELL BEAZLEY

An Hachette UK Company

www.hachette.co.uk

First published in Great Britain in 2014 by
Mitchell Beazley, a division of Octopus Publishing Group Ltd
Endeavour House, 189 Shaftesbury Avenue
London WC2H 8JY
www.octopusbooks.co.uk
www.octopusbooksusa.com

Distributed in the US by Hachette Book Group USA
1290 Avenue of the Americas
4th and 5th Floors, New York, NY 10020

Distributed in Canada by Canadian Manda Group
664 Annette Street, Toronto, Ontario, Canada M6S 2C8

ISBN 978-1-84533-927-2

A CIP catalogue record for this book is available from the British Library

Printed and bound in China

10 9 8 7 6 5 4 3 2

Both metric and imperial measurements are
used in this book. In many cases the figures
given are not precise equivalents, so you
should always use one system or the other
and stick to it; never mix figures from
both systems. Seam allowances are 1.5cm
(⅝in) except where otherwise stated.

Group Publishing Director: Denise Bates
Art Director: Juliette Norsworthy
Editor: Pauline Bache
Design: Miranda Harvey
Photography: Nassima Rothacker
Illustrations: Grace Helmer
Copy Editor: Eleanor van Zandt
Assistant Production Manager: Caroline Alberti

Contents

Introduction

I've known how to sew since I was a child. My mum is a professional dressmaker who worked from home, and she taught me to sew from a young age. Along with a love of sewing I developed a passion for fabric. We always had lots of fabric around, piled high in corners and packed into cupboards. So of course now, in my adult life, it feels completely normal to have fabric lurking in various places around my house, just waiting to be stitched up into the perfect project. I'm a fabric magpie – I buy fabrics even when I don't know at the time exactly what I'll do with them. To me, there is no better souvenir from a holiday or a trip to a new place than some fabric or a length of lovely trim. I like to make things that enable me to see my favourite fabrics every day, in the things that I use and the things that I wear.

As much as I enjoy the actual sewing, for me the really fun part is the planning – having the initial idea, browsing the fabric shops, then working out how something three-dimensional, such as a garment or a bag with secret pockets, for example, goes together. I'll visualize it in my head, then plan the order in which I need to assemble the parts.

It's a challenge, but one I really enjoy; I've never been afraid to give a new idea a try. At the end of the process there's the huge satisfaction of seeing your creations come to life — of making something unique to use, or wear, or give as a present.

Sewing wasn't my first choice of profession: previously I trained and practised as a physiotherapist. But after deciding instead to run my own creative business, I was lucky enough to be chosen to take part in a television competition, *The Great British Sewing Bee*. Having never trained or formally studied the subject, I was keen to accept the challenge of being tested and judged. The whole experience turned out to be so much more than I could have ever dreamed of. I've made amazing new friends, realized that I can do more than I ever thought possible and had so much fun along the way.

Sharing my enthusiasm for sewing is really important for me, so having the chance to write my own book has been so exciting! For this first book I have designed 20 projects, including everything from homewares to accessories and garments. Some are constructed from rectangles that you measure and cut yourself; others use patterns,

provided at the front and back of the book. If you are new to sewing, you'll want to learn the skills introduced in the Techniques section and to try some of the simple projects that will help you build up those skills gradually. Throughout the book you'll find plenty of tips that will help ensure success. For those of you who have some sewing experience already, I hope that the book will provide lots of inspiration as well as new ideas and techniques to try out. I love to experiment and add different twists to the things that I make, so each project has a main version and also a variation, which you can use to spark off your imagination. These variations will show you how easy it is to slightly change a pattern or a project and see a really different effect. Once you see how easy this is, you will be able to make your own designs and interpretations of the projects.

Happy Sewing Everyone!

Techniques

Understanding and Choosing Fabrics

Shopping for fabrics is one of the super-fun parts of sewing. Browsing through fabric shops and seeing all the different colours, prints and textures is always a great source of inspiration for me.

FABRIC FEATURES

There are so many different types and styles of fabric out there that if you're a beginner you may find it a little daunting to choose one for a project. So here's some basic information that may help you.

The first step when considering a fabric is to find out what it is actually made from – that is, its fibre content. It may be woven from a natural fibre, such as cotton, linen, silk or wool, or from rayon (which is manufactured from cellulose, a plant product). Or it may be woven from a synthetic fibre, such as polyester, nylon or spandex. Many fabrics are made from a combination of natural and synthetic fibres, in order to include the best traits of each in terms of weight, drape and care.

The next thing to consider is the weight or type of the fabric. Cotton, for example, comes in many forms. It can be very lightweight, such as a floaty voile or lawn. It can be slightly heavier – for example, quilting-weight cotton, poplin or seersucker. Or heavier still, such as denim. Silk, too, comes in many forms, from very lightweight and smooth, such as crêpe de Chine, to heavier, more structured fabric, such as silk dupion, which has slubs that give it a textured surface.

You can find detailed descriptions of fabric types in books and Internet sites devoted to this subject. Here, I approach the matter on a more practical level, giving you my top tips for choosing a suitable fabric for a project.

❀ **Feel the fabric**. Is it soft and smooth? Does it feel thin or thick? If you are making a garment, would it feel comfortable to wear? If you are making a bag or a cushion cover, would it be durable or would it wear out quickly?

❀ **Check the drape** by holding the fabric up and seeing how it falls. Does it hold its shape firmly or does it float around? Scrunch it up in your hand and see what happens. Does it stay crumpled? Or does it relax into its original shape?

❀ **If the fabric has a pattern**, open it out so you can see the pattern on a large scale. If you are making something small, a large pattern might be broken up too much to be fully seen and appreciated. Try covering up part of the fabric so that you just look at a small area. Does it still look as good?

❀ **If you are making a garment**, see if there is a mirror nearby and hold the fabric up against yourself to try to imagine what it would look like on you. It's easy to fall in love with a bold fabric; but think to yourself, 'Would I love to wear it or would I rather just look at it?'

❀ **Consider how you will take care** of the fabric once you have finished your project. Some fabrics are hand-wash or dry-clean only, check the care symbols on the label. If this information isn't included on the label, check with the sales assistant. Also, some washable fabrics can shrink quite a bit when washed, so it is best practice to prewash and iron your fabric before cutting into it.

✼ **Will the fabric be easy to work with?** Lighter-weight fabrics and slippery or floaty fabrics can be tricky to control when you are sewing, so for your first projects it is best to choose medium- to heavier-weight fabrics.

THE ANATOMY OF A FABRIC

All types of fabric will have certain distinguishing features, which need to be taken into consideration in order to get the best results when you are using them. For one thing, most fabrics will have a right and a wrong side. Sometimes this is really obvious; for example, if a fabric has a printed design, this will look best on the right side, while on the wrong side it will be duller and less clear. This is trickier on a plain fabric; in fact sometimes it's almost impossible to tell the difference. In those situations, once you've decided which will be the right and the wrong side, mark the selvedge on the right side with chalk to make it more obvious as you are working with the fabric, use any kind of mark you like, placing them about 15–20cm (6–8in) apart.

The illustration below shows the significant features of a fabric (see 'Glossary' on page 218).

It's also important to know the width of the fabric. Most fabric comes in one of two main widths: 110–115cm (approx. 43–45in) and 140–150cm (approx. 55–59in). The width of your fabric will determine the amount you need for your project.

STORING FABRIC AND TRIMMINGS

I love collecting fabric, as well as ribbon and other trimmings – often without knowing exactly what I'll do with it. Sometimes I won't use a fabric for months, even years. That's why I like to keep my fabric out on show, so that I can see it all the time. In this way, I'm less likely to forget about it, and can get enjoyment and inspiration from it even when it's just sitting there, still unused. If you haven't got space to display your fabric on a shelf, you can keep a record of what you've got stored away. Staple a swatch of each fabric to a card, on which you then write the pertinent details, such as the width and fibre content and how much of it you've got. Keep your cards in a convenient place – in a box, perhaps, or pinned to your notice board.

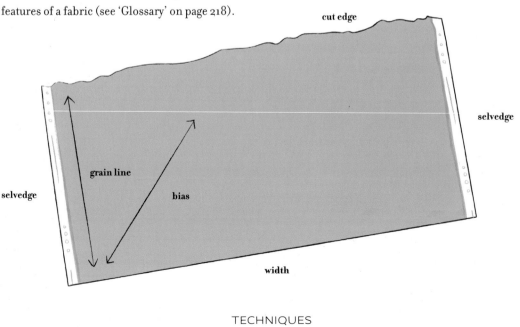

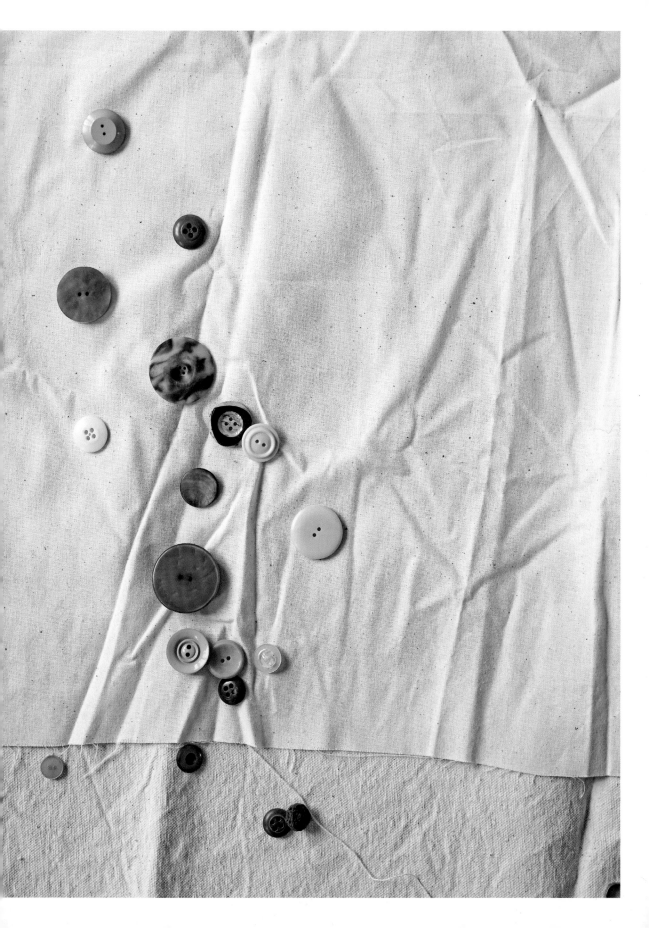

Sewing Equipment

When you first start sewing it will make your life a lot easier if you have the right tools to hand. Buying these can seem like a big investment at first, but once you start sewing you'll quickly realize the benefits of having good-quality supplies.

YOUR SEWING MACHINE

The biggest investment, of course, is your sewing machine. There are many different brands of sewing machine available. Although I can't recommend a specific model, here are the machine features and accessories that I really like and find most useful:

- Needle threader
- Thread cutter
- Ability to do reverse stitching and to change the needle position from one side to another (useful when inserting a zip or piping)
- Variety of stitches and ability to customize them in terms of stitch length and width
- Special buttonhole foot and one-step buttonhole setting
- Ordinary zip foot
- Invisible zip foot
- Blind hem foot
- Walking foot (helps equalize the feed of two layers of fabric – useful when matching up patterns or working with thick fabric)

OTHER EQUIPMENT

- **Tape measure in centimetres and inches** Sewing patterns and tutorials may use either metric or imperial measurements, depending on what part of the world they come from, so it's good to have a measuring tool that gives both types.

- **Seam gauge** This small tool can help you measure small distances accurately.

- **Quilting ruler** This kind of ruler is useful for measuring and drawing straight lines and for cutting fabric squarely.

- **Dressmaking shears** Get a good, sharp pair and use them only for cutting fabric; tie a ribbon around the handle as a reminder!

- **Embroidery scissors** These scissors are useful for making smaller cuts in fabric and cutting threads.

- **Paper scissors** Having these handy will avoid the temptation to use the dressmaking shears on paper.

- **Pinking shears** These are useful for reducing bulk in seams and finishing off raw edges.

- **Rotary cutter and self-healing mat** The cutter is used along with a quilting ruler for cutting clean, sharp lines; the mat is used underneath it to protect your work surface.

- **Hand sewing needles** These come in various lengths, with different-sized eyes; you'll discover which ones you like using for different tasks.

- **Machine needles** These, too, come in different types and sizes; you'll need an assortment for stitching different kinds of fabric.

- **Pins** Long ones with round heads are useful when working with several layers of fabric and are easy to see if they fall on the floor.

- **Pincushion** This is useful for keeping pins and needles to hand.

❀ **Safety pins** Use one of these for pulling elastic through a casing; they're also useful for holding quilt layers together.

❀ **Thimble** You may take a while getting used to it, but this is a must if you are going to do a lot of hand sewing.

❀ **Marking tools** Haberdasheries offer a range of marking tools, including chalk pencils and chalk liners (with the chalk dispensed from a little wheel); you'll soon discover which ones you prefer.

❀ **Bias binding maker** This tool ensures that making your own bias binding is a breeze!

❀ **Rouleau loop turner** This tool is excellent for turning tubes of fabric inside out.

❀ **Seam ripper** I don't think I've ever made anything without using one of these!

❀ **Steam iron** A good steam iron will help give your projects a professional finish.

❀ **Ironing board**

❀ **Pressing cloth** This is useful for protecting delicate fabrics from excess heat or shine from the iron. A piece of lightweight cotton will do the job.

❀ **Sleeve board** This mini ironing board is really useful for pressing tubular garment sections too small to fit over a normal ironing board.

❀ **Dressmakers' pattern paper** This is useful for tracing your size from garment patterns (see page 25). You can also use it for making your own patterns when only the dimensions of fabric to be cut are provided.

❀ **Tracing wheel** This tool can be used to trace the size that you require onto your pattern paper.

❀ **Overlocker (optional)** This machine (also called a serger) will finish seam allowances to a professional standard.

Rouleau loop turner

Seam ripper

Bias binding maker

Marking tools

Rotary cutter

Self-healing mat

Tracing wheel

Sleeve board

Quilting ruler

Seam gauge

Dressmakers' pattern paper

Setting up your Work Space and Sewing Machine

SPACE TO SEW

Having enough space when you sew can make the whole process much, much easier. Although you may not have the luxury of a designated sewing area in your home, you will need to find or make a large, clear space for cutting out. A table is best, but the floor can be used if necessary.

You'll also need a table for your machine. Make sure there is free space around the machine to support the bulk of your project when necessary.

If possible, keep your ironing board and iron set up nearby. You'll need to press seams and other stitching as you complete them, so this will save you time. Sometimes I even use the ironing board as a table when I've run short of space elsewhere.

Protect your dining table, if you're using it for cutting out, with a self-healing mat.

SETTING UP YOUR MACHINE

Although the basic principle of making a stitch is the same from one machine to another, they do vary in their design. Spend some time reading your machine's manual to become familiar with its unique features, so that you can set it up correctly. In particular, make sure that the tension on the top and bobbin threads is balanced, so that the stitches are formed correctly. Follow these tips to make sure you get it right.

❀ To thread the machine, follow the diagram in your sewing machine manual – making sure that you catch the thread around every thread guide.

❀ Wind the bobbin (see page 21) correctly. The bobbin must be wound at tension for the stitches to form properly. Different machines have different ways of achieving this, so consult your manual for specific instructions.

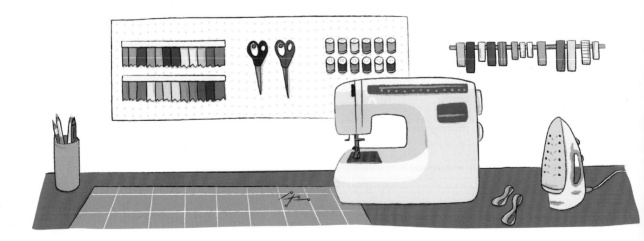

❀ Insert the bobbin correctly. Whether you have a front- or top-loading bobbin, check in your sewing machine manual to see which way it is to be inserted. The direction in which the thread winds off the bobbin affects the tension of the stitches.

❀ Make sure you have the correct type of machine needle for the fabric that you are using. For most fabrics you will use a 'universal' needle, which has a sharp point, but certain fabrics, such as jersey, require a ballpoint needle, which will push between the fabric threads without splitting them.

❀ In terms of needle size, the general rule is: the lighter and finer the fabric, the finer the needle size you'll need. A thick needle in fine fabric can lead to holes where the stitches are formed, a thin needle in thick, heavy fabric leads to a broken needle.

❀ Also make sure that the needle is not blunt; signs of this include puckering of the fabric and incorrect tension, even after you have re-threaded the machine. If you haven't changed your needle recently, try it on a spare piece of fabric before working on your project.

❀ Once the machine is threaded, always check the tension on a scrap of your fabric. The stitches should look the same on each side, as shown in the picture above. If they don't, try re-threading the machine, including re-inserting the bobbin.

❀ If the stitches still look different on each side of the fabric after re-threading, you may have to alter the tension disc on your machine or rewind the bobbin. Your sewing machine manual will tell you how to do this. The most common tension for the machine to be set at is 4, so check that this hasn't accidentally been changed.

Basic Hand Stitches

Although most of your sewing will be on the machine, you will occasionally need to use a sewing needle and thread. In some cases, you may want to hand-tack a seam or a dart before stitching it. Or you may need to join two folded edges invisibly. Here are some basic stitches that will help you do these things.

For most hand stitching a single length of thread works well. There are several kinds of needles; with experience you'll discover which ones suit you best. A thimble will let you push the needle through the fabric – much easier than pulling it, especially if the fabric is thick.

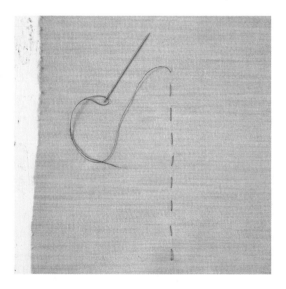

To fasten your thread at the start of your stitching, you can just tie a knot in it. At the end, work two or three backstitches on top of each other to fasten off. You can also use backstitches, instead of a knot, to start your stitching. If the stitching is to be permanent (as opposed to tacking), you should conceal them on the underside of the fabric or in the seam allowance.

◁ RUNNING STITCH/HAND TACKING

This is the simplest type of hand stitch and has many uses. It can be used for gathering a skirt to fit a waistband, for example; for easing a longer edge to fit a slightly shorter one; to hand-quilt (see page 110); or simply as decoration. All you do is fasten your thread (see left), then take the needle in and out of the fabric alternately along the stitching line. For quilting or when used as decoration, the stitches should be even and evenly spaced.

For hand tacking (also called hand basting) the running stitches can be larger and less regular. Hand tacking is used to join two or more sections of fabric together temporarily before you machine-stitch them. This can be useful on very lightweight or slippery fabrics when pins aren't enough to hold the layers in place. It is also required for some special techniques, such as inserting a zip (see page 36). For speed, when doing a long line of tacking, you can pick up several stitches at a time, especially if you use an extra-long needle, such as a straw needle or darner.

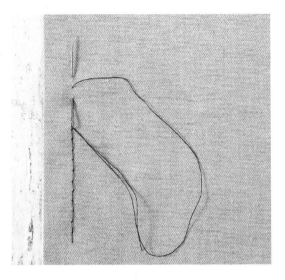

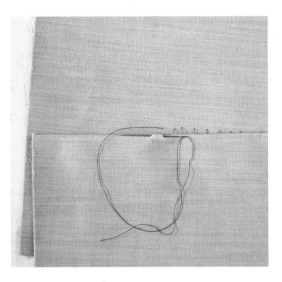

△ BACKSTITCH

As its name implies, this stitch goes backwards as well as forwards! It is much stronger than running stitch and can be used to sew two sections of fabric together permanently and securely.

Fasten your thread, then bring the needle up very slightly ahead of the starting point. Take it back down at the starting point; this makes the first stitch. Bring it up again slightly ahead of the first stitch, then take it down at the end of that stitch. Continue in this way, always bringing the needle up one stitch length ahead and taking it down to meet the previous stitch. The effect on the top of the fabric should resemble machine stitching. On the underside, the stitches overlap each other.

A variation of backstitch, called pickstitch, is more decorative and is sometimes used instead of machine stitching when inserting a zip in a delicate fabric, for example. For this effect, you make your right-side (backwards) stitches very short and space these farther apart – typically about 5mm (¼in). The effect on the right side resembles a row of tiny beads.

△ LADDER STITCH

This invisible method of hand sewing, also known as blind stitch, is a really neat way to join two sections of fabric invisibly. It can be used where two folds of fabric come together or where a fold meets a flat section of fabric.

Fasten your thread and bring the needle up close to the starting point in one section or fold of fabric; insert it directly across in the other section. This makes the first rung of your ladder. Bring the needle up a short way along in the second section and take it across to the first section to make the next rung. Repeat this process, snaking back and forth from one side to the other, gently pulling the thread to bring them together.

To prevent tangles in your thread, run the thread over the edge of a piece of beeswax.

Using Sewing Patterns

Paper patterns form the basis of most sewing projects. When you first start out, they can seem daunting, with all their different lines and symbols. The great thing is, once you learn a few key terms, the symbols and vocabulary are fairly consistent from one pattern manufacturer to another.

PATTERN INFORMATION

A sewing pattern usually comes in an envelope, with illustrations, descriptions and information on the envelope and instructions and the tissue pattern pieces inside. Here are my step-by-step pointers for navigating and interpreting the back of a pattern envelope:

❀ The place to start is the cover of the envelope. Here you may find a few options or variations that are included in the pattern. They are usually identified with letters (A, B, etc.) or numbers (version 1, 2, etc.).

❀ The back of the envelope, with its tables and measurements, can seem a bit overwhelming. However, once you have chosen the version of the pattern you want to make, you can focus on the part of the table you need to look at.

❀ If you are making a garment, the next step is to choose the size you need. Don't just go for the size you normally buy in ready-made clothes – measure yourself. Just as you can take different sizes in different high street shops, you can be different sizes with different pattern manufacturers.

❀ The key areas you'll need to measure are your bust, waist and hips. It is best to measure yourself in your underwear to get the most accurate measurements. Place the tape measure around the largest part of your bust, the smallest part of your waist and the widest part of your hips. Look in the mirror as you do this, as quite often people don't measure high enough for the waist or low enough for the hips. Stay relaxed and don't pull the tape measure too tight, but at the same time make sure it is lying flat against your body.

❀ Match your measurements up to the sizes on the pattern envelope to choose your size. If you don't fit one size you will have to alter the pattern slightly. This may be a relatively simple matter. Pattern pieces are normally printed with several size lines; you cut along the line for your size. So you could merge your own size line at the side seams to accommodate the variation. Or the alteration could be more complex – for example, adjusting for a relatively full or small bust. See the recommended reading list in 'Inspiration' on page 219 for more guidance on this.

❀ Once you know what size you'll be making, you can find out how much fabric you'll need. There will usually be two choices, depending on the width of your chosen fabric. The pattern will also recommend the types of fabric suitable for the design and will list any haberdashery items that you need, such as buttons, zips or elastic.

CUTTING OUT YOUR FABRIC

To get the best results it's really important to cut out accurately, following the grain of the fabric (see page 14). Here are some points to bear in mind.

1 If your fabric is washable, prewash and iron it, then lay it out on a flat surface, folded in half, with the right sides of the fabric together (so you'll be working on the wrong side) and the selvedges aligned. It is worth spending a bit of time making sure that the fabric lies straight and flat.

2 It is also worth ironing your pattern pieces (use a cool iron) to get them nice and flat; this will increase your accuracy when cutting out your fabric.

3 Your pattern will include a cutting layout. This is like a map, showing you where the different pattern pieces should be set out on the fabric. Make sure to choose the correct layout for your size and fabric width. While you're still a beginner, it's best to follow the layout, but with more experience you'll have the confidence to alter the layout to minimize fabric wastage; layouts can be over generous with space and it can feel like you are wasting a lot of fabric. But don't be tempted to buy less than the recommended amount of fabric, as you could run short! Just keep any left-over fabric and use it for another project – maybe patchwork, doll clothes or bias binding (see page 50).

4 If you are using a printed fabric with a one-way design – for example, flowers with stems – you will need to make sure that the pattern pieces all line up in the right direction, so that you don't end up with some or all of the garment sections upside down.

5 The next step is ensuring that you position the pieces correctly in relation to the fabric grain.

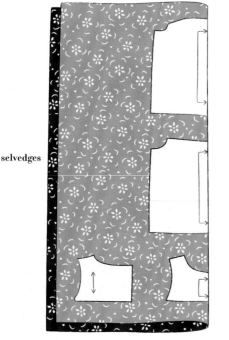

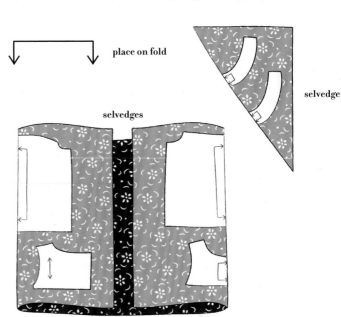

place on straight of grain (lengthways)

place on fold

selvedge

selvedges

selvedges

The pattern will be marked with symbols to help you do this. If a piece is to be placed on a fold, that edge of the pattern will be clearly marked; if it is to be cut double, there will be an arrow, or simply a straight line, which needs to be lined up parallel to the selvedge.

6 Next you will need to pin the pattern onto the fabric. First pin each piece correctly along the fold line or straight grain line (see page 14). Then place pins around the edge of each pattern piece, smoothing out the pattern pieces and fabric as you go. Place the pins close to the edge of the pattern pieces but not so close that they stick out over the edge. If your fabric is quite lightweight or slippery, you will need more pins. You will also need more pins around curved areas.

7 Refine your pinning technique! Try to keep the pattern pieces and fabric as flat as you can while pinning, so both hands stay on top of the fabric at all times. I find it easiest to hold the pin at the head, like a little lever, then push it through the fabric, using the 'lever' movement (see photograph a) to pick the fabric up. Using your other hand to hold the fabric as flat as possible, push the pin through (see photograph b).

8 When cutting out, take nice big cuts on long, straight pieces and make smaller cuts on the curves.

9 If you have a thin section of fabric to cut off (and you are right-handed) orient the fabric and pattern so that the thin section of fabric is on your left-hand side (see photograph c). Grip it between your thumb and index finger, and as you cut, pull it gently towards you to create some tension. This makes it much easier to cut an accurate line.

a Use the pin to pick the fabric up in a 'lever' movement

b Use your other hand to hold the fabric as flat as possible

c Create tension to cut an accurate line

PATTERN SYMBOLS

⟵————⟶

Straight grain line This must be parallel to the selvedge. Measure between them at several points to make sure that they are parallel.

Fold line The edge of the pattern piece needs to line up with where your fabric is folded. Squash your fabric flat at the fold to make sure it's accurate.

▼ ▼ ▼

Notches These little triangles are important when you sew seams. They are single or in groups of two or three. Make sure you mark all of the notches.

○

Dots These marks are also important for putting your project together accurately. They are used for a variety of things including pocket placement guides, the start and end of gathering stitches, or the end of a zip.

Darts These (see page 48) help to shape fitted garments. They can be single or double pointed.

⊢—✕—⊣

Buttonholes A short line indicates the buttonhole itself (see page 41); the 'x' marks the button.

◉

Buttons This mark is used to position a button on a project where there is no buttonhole (see 'Ribbon Handbag' on page 195).

TRANSFERRING PATTERN MARKINGS

Once you have cut out your fabric, you need to transfer the pattern markings onto your fabric. It's important to go through each pattern piece methodically and check that you haven't missed anything, so that it will be much easier to put the project together later.

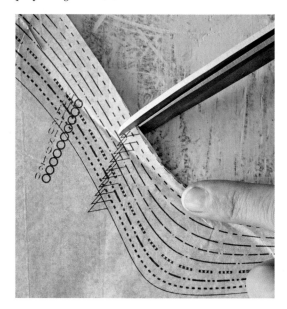

△ **Notches can be marked** by cutting a small triangle in the fabric, or simply with a little slit, as shown above. Take care not to cut too deeply into the seam allowance – about 1cm (³⁄₈in) is adequate.

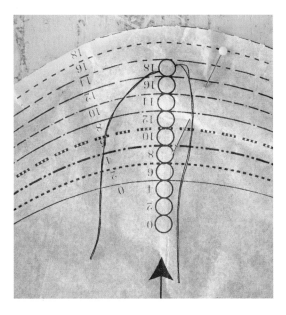

△ **Dots or circles can be marked** with tailor's tacks or with chalk. A tailor's tack is a single stitch at the point of the mark which goes through all layers of fabric. Use a doubled thread and make a single stitch through the mark, leaving a thread tail of about 5cm (2in) and cutting off the thread to the same length. (Leave longer tails if you are working through more than two layers of fabric.) When you separate the fabric layers take care not to pull the top layer free of the tack, then cut the threads between the two layers so that both layers are marked with the thread.

△ **To transfer markings with chalk**, remove the pins that are holding your pattern to your fabric, but keep the pattern lined up with the edges of your fabric. Peel back the pattern to the point of the marking, then draw the dot, or other marking, on the fabric with the chalk. To mark the other fabric layer, remove the pattern, turn the fabric over, place the pattern piece on top, aligning it carefully with the fabric edges, and mark again as shown.

Seams

A seam is the joining of two or more layers of fabric. There are different types of seams and different ways to finish them.

SEAM ALLOWANCES

The distance between the stitching line and the raw edge is called the seam allowance. Usually this is 1.5cm (⅝in); most of the projects in this book use this seam allowance, except where otherwise stated. Other patterns may include a 1.2cm (½in) seam allowance; and in quilting and patchwork projects the standard seam allowance is 5–6mm (¼in). Always check pattern instructions to find the seam allowance, as this will ensure that the finished object is the right size.

Once you know the correct seam allowance, it's important to stick to it, so that your stitching line is straight. There are several ways to do this. One way is to find the appropriate marking on the foot plate of your machine and make sure that the raw edge is always lined up with that mark.

Alternatively, mark the stitching line on the fabric using a seam gauge and chalk before you sew the seam. This is especially useful when sewing a curved seam (see photograph a). Or you can put some coloured tape on the foot plate to align with the fabric edges (see photograph b).

With practice you will learn what the correct seam allowance looks like; on my machine, I know how much fabric extends on the right-hand side of the presser foot for a 1.5cm (⅝in) seam allowance.

TO PRACTISE STITCHING STRAIGHT SEAMS, MAKE THE ENVELOPE CUSHION COVER (PAGE 68).

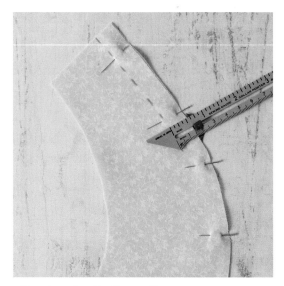

a *Measuring and marking the seam allowance*

b *Ensure you stick to the correct seam allowance*

PLAIN SEAM

This is the simplest kind of seam and is the most often used. Practise it on medium-weight cotton, which is easy to work with, to give yourself confidence in using the basic techniques.

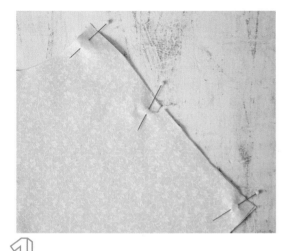

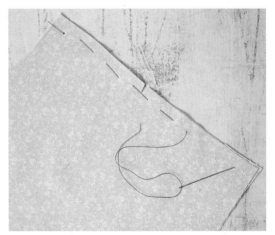

1 PIN THE PIECES TOGETHER

First cut out the pieces as accurately as possible, following the pattern, and transfer any markings onto the fabric (see page 28). Place the pieces together with right sides facing. Match up any notches or other markings, and pin the pieces together at those points. Next, pin the start and end of the seam. Finally, pin the rest of the seam together. The number of pins you need will depend partly on how slippery your fabric is or whether the seam is straight or curved.

2 HAND-TACK THE SEAM

Although this step is not always necessary, you may want to hand-tack the pieces together after pinning (see page 22). You can then remove the pins and stitch the seam. Tack just outside the stitching line; if you tack directly over it, you'll have a tedious job later removing bits of tacking thread from the machine stitching.

Inserting pins When you sew the seam, you will need to take the pins out as you go. Stitching over pins can cause the needle to become blunt or break and can also distort the stitching. When you stitch, the raw edge will always be on your right-hand side. So you can insert the pins either parallel to the edge, with the head of the pin towards you, or perpendicular to it, head to the right, for easy removal while you stitch.

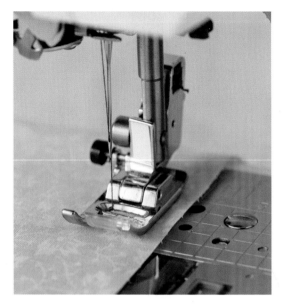

③ MACHINE-STITCH THE SEAM

Place the fabric on the foot plate at the correct position (see 'Seam Allowances', page 30) and lower the needle into it at the beginning of your stitching line. Set the machine for straight stitch at your chosen stitch length (usually 2.5mm [10 stitches per inch]). Stitch forwards for 3 or 4 stitches, then reverse to the starting point; this locks the stitches so they won't come loose. Now stitch forwards to the end, reverse as before, then stitch to the end again. Cut off the thread and remove the tacking stitches, if any.

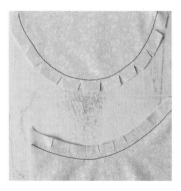

Clipping/notching seam allowances is a way to decrease the bulk in the seam allowance and to help the curve lie properly. On convex (outward) curves you will need to notch the seam allowance by cutting small triangles in it; these will close up when the piece is turned right side out. On concave (inward) curves you will need to make small snips in the seam allowance to help it stretch around the curve. The tighter the curve, the more clips or notches you will need.

Stitching around corners and curves. When you have to stitch around a corner, simply keep the needle in the fabric, lift the presser foot and pivot your work to the correct position. Lower the presser foot and continue stitching.

To get a nice, even seam allowance around a curve, try marking the stitching line with chalk, as shown on page 30, until you get used to judging it by eye. You may have to lift the presser foot at times and very slightly pivot your work in order to maintain the curve. Or try a slightly shorter stitch; this will help you produce a more gradual curve.

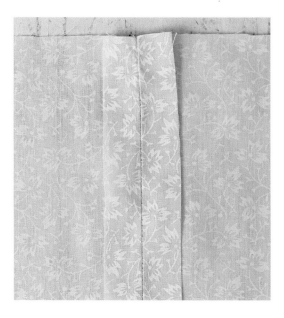

 PRESS THE SEAM

First of all, using a steam iron, press the seam flat, without opening it, to set the stitches into the fabric. Then press the seam allowances open, as shown, unless instructed otherwise by the pattern. Sometimes the seam allowances need to be pressed to one side or the other; the pattern instructions will state this.

Pressing and ironing are different! To press, you place the iron on your fabric and apply gentle pressure, moving it only slightly, if at all, then lift it off; repeat on adjacent areas, if necessary. Using steam will help this process. Pressing is best suited to areas where you need to be precise. To iron, you move the iron back and forth over your fabric; this is used on a larger area of fabric, in order to smooth it.

When ironing or pressing fabric on the right side, it's best to use a pressing cloth. This protects the fabric from any residue on the iron and helps reduce the chance of a shine appearing on it. Always test the iron temperature on a scrap of your fabric.

5 FINISH OFF THE SEAM ALLOWANCES

You normally need to treat the raw edges to prevent them from fraying (which weakens the seam). The finish you choose will depend on the type of fabric that you are using and what you are making, as well as your own personal preferences.

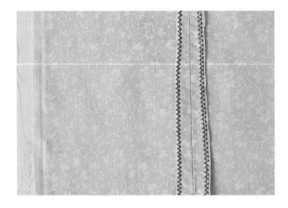

△ **Zigzag stitch** Most machines will do a zigzag stitch, which can be set for different lengths and widths; practise on a scrap of your fabric to determine the best setting for it. Stitch close to the raw edge of the seam allowance.

△ **Bound seam finish** This uses bias binding (see page 50) to cover the raw edges. It adds extra bulk to the seam so isn't suitable for very lightweight fabrics, but it's a lovely way to add colour and contrast. Simply sandwich the raw edge between the folded binding and stitch into place.

△ **Straight stitch and pinking shears** On each seam allowance stitch an extra line of straight stitch and then trim the edge with pinking shears. The zigzag edge they cut is resistant to fraying.

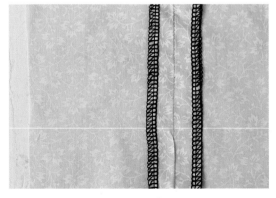

△ **Overlocker/serger** This separate machine uses 3 or 4 threads at the same time to sew a special stitch that binds the raw edge.

FRENCH SEAM

This is my favourite type of seam, as it ends up narrower than a plain seam and hides all the raw edges on the inside, so it looks really neat. However it does add some bulk at the seamline so is better for light- to medium-weight fabrics.

1 STITCH THE FIRST SEAM

With wrong sides of the fabric together, stitch a seam taking only 5mm (¼in) seam allowance. Then trim the edges close to the stitching.

2 PRESS THE SEAM

First press the seam flat as usual, then open out the fabric and press the trimmed seam allowances to one side, as shown. Now fold the fabric so that the right sides are facing and press the seam flat. (See 'To get a crisp pressed edge' on page 71.)

3 STITCH THE SECOND SEAM

Stitch again, 5mm (¼in) from the first seam, enclosing the raw edges. Press this seam flat, then to one side or the other as instructed by the pattern.

Inserting a Zip

Zips are probably the most common fastening used in garments, and they are also used for bags, purses and soft furnishings. Inserting a zip can be done in several different ways. If you've never inserted a zip before, the process may look complicated, but I promise it isn't as scary as it seems.

STANDARD CENTRED INSERTION

This is the simplest way to insert a zip. It's neat and works well in most garments and accessories.

1 MACHINE-TACK THE ZIP OPENING

Mark the start and end of the opening with chalk on the right and wrong sides of the fabric on both of the pieces to be joined. Pin the sections together with right sides facing, then use a long machine stitch (4mm [⅛in]), to close the opening, taking 1.5cm (⅝in) seam allowance. Stitch the rest of the seam with a normal-length stitch, reversing at beginning and end as usual. Press the seam allowances open. It is a good idea to finish off the raw edges of the seam at this point.

PRACTISE THIS BASIC ZIP TECHNIQUE ON THE 'TRIMMED CUSHION COVER' (SEE PAGE 120) OR THE 'PICK YOUR POCKETS SKIRT' (SEE PAGE 188).

2 HAND-TACK THE ZIP IN PLACE

Place the closed zip on top of the seam allowances with the teeth facing down and directly over the tacked opening. Pin and then hand-tack the zip in place along both edges. You will have to open the zip slightly before tacking the upper edges to get the slider out of the way. This allows the tops of the zip tape to sit closer together, so that the zip will close neatly once it is sewn in place. Once the zip is tacked, remove the pins.

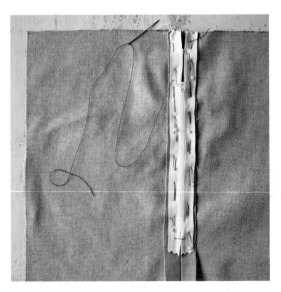

3 STITCH THE ZIP IN PLACE

Unpick the machine tacking stitches used to close the zip (allowing you to move the slider up and down when you are sewing).

With the zip foot on your machine and the right side of the fabric facing up, stitch the zip in place about 1cm (⅜in) from the seamline (draw a chalk line as a guide first). Sew about 5cm (2in) down, stop with the needle in the fabric, lift the presser foot then move the zip slider out of the way. Lower the presser foot again and continue. When you reach the chalk mark at the bottom, lift the presser foot, pivot the work 90 degrees and stitch across the bottom of the zip, then pivot again and stitch up the other side. Remember to reverse-stitch at the start and end of the your line of stitching. Using a seam ripper, unpick the tacking stitches.

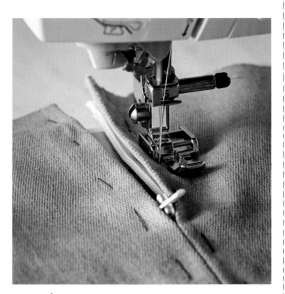

INVISIBLE ZIP INSERTION

This method (also called a 'concealed zip') is my favourite way to insert a zip, as it gives such a nice neat finish on the outside. It is a little trickier than the standard zip insertion, and unlike that method, this one involves inserting the zip first, then stitching the rest of the seam. You'll need to buy a special invisible zip foot for your machine.

1 IRON YOUR ZIP!

I know it sounds a little strange, but you need to do this in order to stitch close enough to the teeth of the zip – and that's what makes it invisible.

Open the zip and, working on the wrong side and using a cool iron (so the teeth don't melt!), press the teeth towards the opening of the zip.

2 PIN AND TACK THE ZIP TO THE FABRIC

Place the two fabric pieces right side up alongside each other. Open the zip and place it right side up between them; make sure it isn't twisted. Now turn the left-hand section of the zip over onto the left-hand fabric piece, with their right sides facing. Ensure that the top of the zip tape is aligned with the raw edge of the fabric and that the inner edge of the teeth lies 1.5cm (⅝in) from the opening edge of the fabric. Pin, then tack the zip in place down to about 2cm (¾in) from the bottom of the teeth. Turn the right-hand side of the zip over and pin and tack it to the other section in the same way.

3 STITCH THE ZIP IN PLACE

The invisible zip foot has two small grooves in the bottom. The teeth of the zip will fit into these grooves, which will hold the teeth back so that you can stitch right next to them. Start stitching at the top of one side of the zip (remember to reverse-stitch) and continue along the length of the zip, making sure that the teeth stay upright and feed into the foot properly. You may have to gently roll the teeth with your fingers to guide them under the foot. The stitching should be close to the teeth, but take care not to stitch on top of them, which would, of course, make the zip unusable. So if you think you're too close, just stop, take the work out and have a look.

Stitch as close as you can to the bottom of the zip; you won't get all the way down. Then stitch the zip along the other side, again starting at the top.

WINDOW ZIP INSERTION

This type of zip insertion makes more of a feature of the zip, so is often used when adding a pocket to a bag, for example.

1 TRANSFER THE MARKINGS AND CUT THE WINDOW

On the wrong side of your main fabric, using tailor's chalk and a ruler (preferably a quilting ruler, for ease and accuracy), mark a line the same length as the zip teeth. Now mark a narrow rectangle around this, 1.2–1.5cm (1/2–5/8in) wide and 1.5cm (5/8in) longer than the centre line. Make sure the first line is exactly centred. (If you are using a pattern you can simply transfer the marks printed on it.)

Cut a rectangle of lightweight iron-on interfacing, large enough to cover all of the markings (the chalk lines will be visible), and iron this onto the wrong side of the fabric.

Using embroidery scissors, cut open this window along the central line, then cut diagonally to the corners at both ends. Press these flaps back along the lines towards the wrong side of the fabric.

Repeat these steps on the pocket lining piece.

4 SEW THE SEAM BELOW THE ZIP

Check that the zip works. If it gets stuck you may have sewn too close to the teeth in places. The stitching will have to be unpicked and resewn.

If all is well, close the zip and place the right sides of the fabric together. Sandwich the zip in the seam allowance and push the bottom of the zip out to the side, so that it won't get caught in the rest of the seam. Pin the rest of the seam together. Attach a normal zip foot to your machine and stitch the rest of the seam, starting at the bottom edge and stitching as close as possible to the stitching used to attach the zip. You may wish to hand-tack the seam first to make sure it meets the zip opening smoothly. Remember to secure the stitching with some reverse stitches. Press the seam open.

PRACTISE THIS TECHNIQUE ON THE 'HAVE IT YOUR WAY DRESS' (SEE PAGE 200).

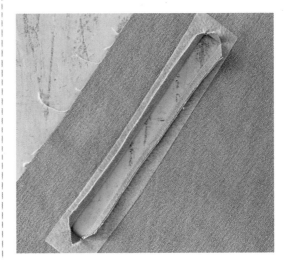

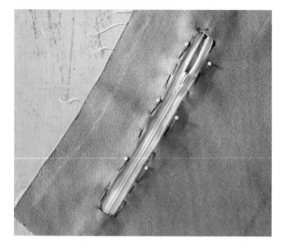

2 PIN AND TACK THE ZIP TO THE OPENING

Place the fabric right side up over the zip so that the zip is centred in the window. Pin then hand-tack the zip in place, close to the turned-under edge. Remove the pins.

TRY OUT THIS TECHNIQUE ON THE 'BIG WEEKEND BAG' (SEE PAGE 146).

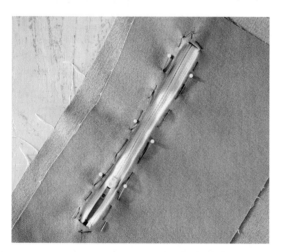

3 PIN AND TACK THE POCKET LINING IN PLACE

Turn the main fabric piece wrong side up. Place the lining piece on top, with its window exposing the zip, and pin. Then hand-tack this to the zip tape to hold it securely in place. (The stitches need not go through all the layers.)

4 STITCH THE ZIP IN PLACE

With an ordinary zip foot attachment, topstitch the zip in place close to the folded edge, going through the main fabric, the zip tape and the pocket lining at the same time. Remove the tacking stitches. (You may need to stitch over the tacking in places, but these threads can be removed with a seam ripper.)

In some patterns you may be instructed to attach another lining section to the one that is attached to the zip (to form a pocket); specific instructions for this will be provided.

Buttons and Other Fastenings

For most people, sewing on a button presents no problems; buttonholes are another matter – though, like zips, they're easier than you may think.

MAKING A BUTTONHOLE

For a long time I thought buttonholes were too complicated even to attempt. The traditional hand-stitched buttonhole is almost a craft in itself and takes a lot of practice to get right. Then I discovered that my machine had a handy buttonhole setting and that actually it's not complicated at all.

As you know, a buttonhole is basically a slit cut in the fabric for a button to pass through. If you were just to cut a slit in the fabric, though, it would fray and get bigger. You must reinforce the buttonhole with stitching. You can do this by machine, using a very tight zigzag stitch, before cutting the opening.

Most modern machines have a buttonhole setting. The basic machines typically have a four-step buttonhole setting which requires you to control the size of the buttonhole while it's stitching. Swankier machines have a one-step buttonhole setting that automatically stitches the correct size buttonhole for the size of your button. As all machines work slightly differently, it's best to look in your manual for specific instructions on sewing a buttonhole.

Here are my top tips for ensuring a successful, strong buttonhole:

❀ Take care to transfer the pattern's buttonhole markings accurately (see page 28), using a chalk pencil. Buttonhole stitching can be tricky to unpick, so it's best to get it in the right place first time.

❀ Make sure that the buttonhole is big enough for your button! The length of the buttonhole should be the diameter or width of the button, plus the thickness of the button, as indicated by the arrows (see photograph b). At each end of the buttonhole there will be a bar tack: stitching that goes across both sides of the buttonhole. Remember that the actual length of the buttonhole will lie between these.

❀ Check that you have the correct tension on the machine by doing a practice buttonhole. Use the same fabric layers that you will be stitching through on your garment, including any interfacing or lining.

❀ To cut open your buttonhole, first place a pin at one end, just before one of the bar tacks. Using a seam ripper, push up towards the pin, as shown below, which will stop you from slipping and cutting through the stitching.

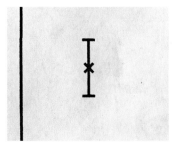

a *Buttonhole pattern marking*

b *Measuring your button*

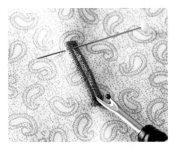

c *Cutting open your buttonhole*

PRACTISE YOUR BUTTONHOLE AND BUTTON SKILLS ON THE YOKE TOP (PAGE 180).

SEWING ON A BUTTON

It's easy enough to sew on a button, but there is a way to do it nice and securely. Here are my top tips:

✿ Use a double thread – about 40cm (15in) long when doubled.

✿ Run the strands through some beeswax; this will help to strengthen the thread and prevent it from knotting while stitching.

✿ Anchor the thread with two or three backstitches (see page 23) on the right side of the fabric at the point where the button is to be attached.

Shank buttons For attaching this kind of button, you alternately take the needle through the hole in the shank and then through the fabric, making a stitch no longer than the thickness of the shank. About eight stitches should be enough.

Sew-through buttons Some of these have two holes; others have four. If your button has four holes, work diagonally across them, four or five times in one direction, then the same number of times in the other.

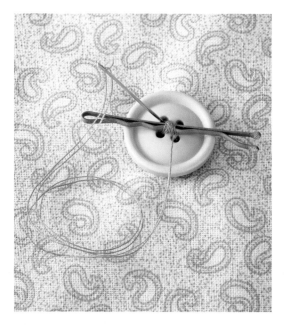

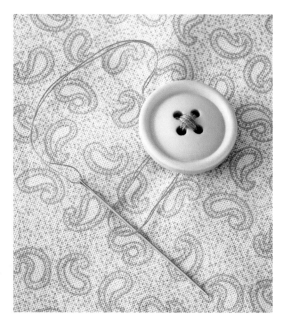

△ **Making a thread shank on sew-through buttons** If your fabric is very thick, you may want to create a bit of slack in the stitches so that the button can sit slightly proud of the fabric. To do this place a thick needle or hairgrip over the button and stitch over that. Then remove the hair grip before fastening off the thread.

△ **Fastening off the thread** Bring the thread to the right side of the fabric but underneath the button. Wrap it around the stitches about five times. To knot the thread, hold back a loop with your finger and wrap the thread around again, then pass the needle through the loop and pull tight; repeat this once or twice more.

OTHER FASTENINGS

There are several other types of fastenings used in sewing projects, and they come in a variety of different sizes and finishes to blend in with your fabric. Your pattern should tell you what type of fastening you would need.

✿ **A hook and bar** are commonly used to fasten trousers at the waistband.

✿ **A hook and eye** (basically a curved version of a bar) are often used just above a zip, to ensure that it will not slide open.

✿ **Press studs** (also called snaps) are used in a variety of situations – sometimes as a substitute for buttons and buttonholes. Some are sewn on; others are inserted using a punch and die with a hammer.

✿ **Magnetic studs** are commonly used in making bags. Some of them can be sewn on; others have metal tabs for attaching them to the fabric. When attaching this kind, you'll have to reinforce the fabric with some iron-on interfacing and then cut two small slits in the fabric for the tabs to go through. Bend the tabs inwards to secure the stud.

magnetic studs

hook and bar

hook and eye

press studs

Sewing on fastenings As for buttons, use a double thread and run it through beeswax for extra strength. Fasten the thread with two or three backstitches and work through each hole several times.

Hems

A hem is basically a way to hide the lower raw edges of a garment.
You can do this invisibly, or you can make the hem a feature.
Here are my preferred ways of doing hems.

DOUBLE FOLD HEM: TOPSTITCHED

The double fold hem is the standard hem used in dressmaking. The depth of the
finished hem will vary according to the style of garment and the fabric. Your pattern
will usually state the hem allowance. A narrow hem may be 5mm–1.2cm (¼–½in)
deep, whereas a deeper hem may be 2.5–4cm (1–1½in) deep or even more. This
deeper hem will add weight to the bottom of the garment, whereas a narrower hem will
be lighter and allow the garment to float a little. The instructions that follow are for a
topstitched hem. This is the quickest and most straightforward method of finishing a
hem, but the line of stitching will be visible, so you need to make sure it is even.

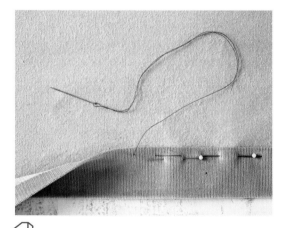

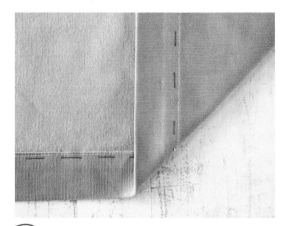

1 TURN UP THE HEM

Turn up the hem allowance on your chosen hemline
and press the fold. Trim the hem allowance if
necessary, then turn under the raw edge and press
again. On the hem shown, the depth is 4cm (1½in),
plus another 1.2cm (½in) folded inside. Pin the
folded edge in place, then hand-tack it as shown
and remove the pins.

2 TOPSTITCH THE HEM

Place the garment right side up on the machine.
Lower the needle into the hem close to the top of
the fold. Then lower the presser foot and begin
stitching (without reverse-stitching this time). Use
a guideline or marker on your machine to ensure
that you stitch at a consistent distance away from
the lower edge all the way around. When you reach
the starting point, overlap the stitching by two or
three stitches to fasten it.

DOUBLE FOLD INVISIBLE HEM

Although more time consuming than a topstitched hem, this invisible hand-stitched method, using catch stitch (also called herringbone stitch) gives a really slick finish.

First turn up and hand-tack the hem as described on page 44. Work the tacking at least 5mm (¼in) down from the fold, which you will need to pull open a little.

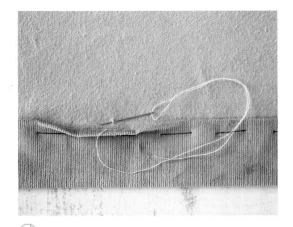

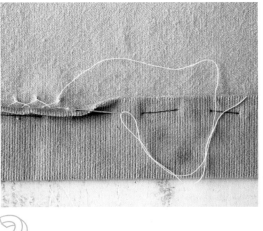

1 BEGIN THE STITCHING

Work with a single strand of thread. Knot the end and bring the needle up through the folded edge, Turn back the hem to thread your needle through the fold, which hides the knot. (Or, if you prefer, fasten the thread with a few backstitches.) As you sew, you will be working from left to right along the hem but will have the needle pointing towards the left. (Reverse this if you are left-handed.) Sew a very small stitch into the main fabric, catching in only a few threads; this should ensure that you don't see the stitch from the other side.

2 CONTINUE THE STITCHING

Move along to the right a little – about 5mm (¼in) – and make a small stitch in the fold of the hem. Then move along to the right the same distance and make another stitch into the main fabric. Continue in this way all around the hem. You will notice that the threads cross over slightly and look like little X's; when the fold is turned up they are hidden. Secure the thread with a few backstitches.

Use a seam gauge, if you like (see page 17), to measure the depth of the hem as you press it up and ensure that it is even all the way around.

MACHINE-STITCHED INVISIBLE HEM

Some sewing machines have a 'blind hem' setting (often used with a special foot). This, too, produces a hem that is invisible from the right side, although the stitches are visible on the inside. For this type of hem only a single fold is made, and the raw edge is simply finished in some way (see page 34), so it is slightly less bulky than a double fold hem. Check your sewing machine manual for how to use the blind hem setting.

BOUND HEM

This method of hemming uses bias binding and will make a feature of the hem, so choose binding that contrasts with your main fabric. You can buy ready-made bias binding or make your own (see page 50). You will need enough binding to go all the way around your hem plus another 10cm (4in) for joining the ends.

1 PIN THE BINDING TO THE HEM EDGE

Trim the hem edge to your chosen length and even it if necessary (see page 47). Open out one edge of the bias binding and place this, right side down, against the wrong side of the fabric edge with raw edges aligned. Pin it in place.

2 STITCH THE BINDING IN PLACE

Machine-stitch along the fold line of the bias binding, leaving about 5cm (2in) free at the start. Continue around the hem, stopping 3cm (1in) from where you began. Join the ends of the binding (see page 54). Continue the stitching over the join to meet the starting point; fasten off.

Fixing your hemline On many garments you can simply decide how much hem allowance you want – or use the one marked on the pattern – then turn up the hem and finish it. But sometimes you'll want to adjust the length, making the garment shorter (patterns are normally sized for tall people). Or the lower edge may need straightening – perhaps to allow for your individual figure. Turn up the suggested hem allowance and pin it in place, then try on the garment. If possible, ask someone to help you make any adjustments. Remove the garment and mark the foldline with pins along the edge. Press the fold, then mark the hem allowance, trim if necessary and complete the hem.

3 PRESS THE SEAM

Press the binding over the seam, away from the fabric, as shown. Now turn the garment right side up and and press the binding over the fabric edge along the seamline, enclosing the raw edges, so that the binding is exposed.

4 TOPSTITCH THE HEM

Pin the binding in place, then topstitch it to the fabric close to its upper and lower edges.

Darts

Darts are used in garment making to provide shape and make a garment more fitted. It is a fold in the fabric that is stitched in place. Once a dart is sewn in place the flat fabric you started with becomes three-dimensional. Darts are commonly found at the bust, where they are single-pointed. They are also used around the waistline at the front and back of garments, where they can be double-pointed.

The steps below explain how to insert a single-pointed dart once you have cut out your fabric following a pattern, but while the pattern is still pinned to the fabric.

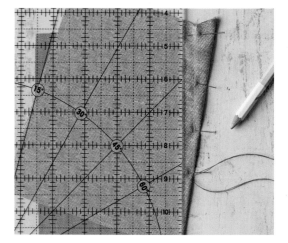

1 MARK THE DART

Put a few extra pins around the dart to ensure the fabric stays against the pattern – especially important if you have lightweight or slippery fabric. At the point of the dart sew a very small stitch through the tissue and both layers of fabric, leaving two long tails of thread (this is a tailor's tack). At the wide starting points of the dart, make a small snip in the fabric, as if you were marking a notch.

Note – if you are sewing a double-pointed dart, use more tailor's tacks to mark several points along the path of the dart instead of making notches.

2 PREPARE THE DART FOR SEWING

Remove the pattern, being careful not to remove the tailor's tack. Fold the dart with right sides of the fabric facing, so that the two notches match up at the edge, and pin in place. Move the fabric so the tailor's tack is lying on the fold. Flatten out the fabric and pin in place.

Mark a stitch guide line with chalk by placing a ruler between the notches at the edge and the tailor's tack at the point of the dart.

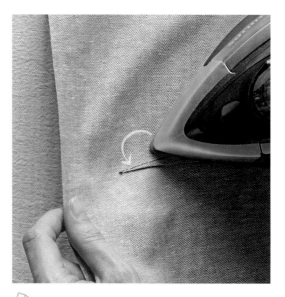

3 SEW THE DART

Starting at the wide edge of the dart, stitch over your chalk line, with a reverse stitch at the beginning. Gradually merge the line of stitching towards the point of the dart so that the last few stitches are very close but parallel to the fold. Don't reverse stitch at the point of the dart, but instead leave long tails of thread that you can then tie in a knot. This prevents excess bulk at the point.

Note – if you are sewing a double-pointed dart, start stitching in the widest centre section of the dart and work out to the two points separately.

4 PRESS THE DART

This step makes the difference between a good dart and a pointy one. First of all, press the dart with the fabric flat to set the stitches into the fabric. Then open out the fabric so that the right side of the fabric faces the ironing board and the dart flap is facing upwards. Use the edge of the iron to press the dart in the direction specified in the pattern (usually downwards for bust darts) and work your way towards the point. Gently lift the fabric up at the point of the dart and, using the tip of the iron, move in a circular motion over the point to round it out. You could spray it with water to remove any creases at the point. This will make the point of the dart melt and blend in smoothly.

Bias Binding

Bias binding is great to add little details and decorative touches. You can use ready-made binding or make your own to hide raw edges of seams, highlight a hem or pocket opening, strengthen necklines or armholes, or as decorative piping.

Bias binding is so called because it is cut at a 45-degree angle to the straight grain of the fabric. This makes it more pliable and gives maximum elasticity for stretching it around corners and curves – plenty of those in dressmaking!

I prefer to make my own bias binding because in this way I can give my sewing projects a uniquely personal touch. Also, quite often ready-made bias binding is a little stiff or rough, due to the coating put on it to help it keep its shape on the roll. When you make your own, from a lovely soft cotton lawn, for example, it just feels so much nicer!

There are two methods for making bias binding. The continuous method makes one very long length of binding. It is useful for when you have extra-long edges to bind or if you know you'll use that particular fabric a lot in future projects. The single length, piecing method will make shorter lengths, but it is quicker; so if you just have a small section to bind and want to get on with it, this method is more suitable.

EQUIPMENT YOU WILL NEED TO MAKE YOUR OWN BIAS BINDING:

❧ **square of dressmakers' pattern paper** 50 x 50cm (20 x 20in)

❧ **quilting ruler**, 60cm (24in), or an ordinary long ruler

❧ **tailors' chalk pencil**

❧ **bias binding maker** in your desired size. I use the 18mm and 25mm (approx. ¾in and 1in) sizes most often. It is possible to make bias binding without one of these, but I find it quite fiddly and very hard to get even.

MAKING BIAS TAPE: SINGLE LENGTH METHOD

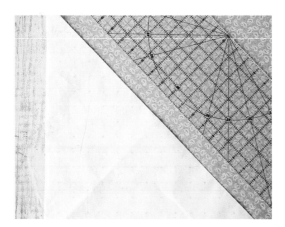

1 MARK THE BIAS LINE

Cut a rectangle of fabric measuring 55cm (22in) along the selvedge by the width of your fabric. Place the paper square along the selvedge, then fold it in half diagonally so that you have a triangle. Using your ruler and chalk, mark a line on your fabric following the diagonal edge of the triangle; this is the bias line.

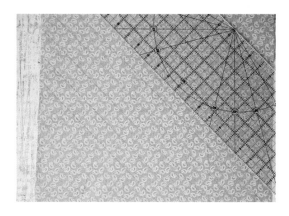

2 MARK AND CUT THE STRIPS

Following the bias line you've marked, draw more lines parallel to it at the correct width for your bias binding maker. (Refer to the packaging for a size guide.) Cut out your strips along the lines you have drawn. A rotary cutter and self-healing mat (see page 17), used alongside the ruler, will make this job quicker. Square off the ends of the strips.

3 JOIN THE STRIPS

Place two strips together with right sides facing at 90 degrees to each other, to make a square corner. Sew the strips together along the diagonal as shown. Trim the seam allowances to about 1cm (3⁄8in) and press the seam open. Repeat for the remaining strips to make the required length of binding and use a bias binding maker (see page 53) to turn the bias binding tape into bias binding.

MAKING BIAS TAPE: CONTINUOUS METHOD

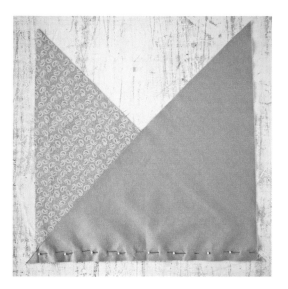

1 CONSTRUCT THE BASIC SHAPE

Using paper pattern, mark and cut out a square of fabric along the selvedge. This can be any size, but 50cm (20in) square is a useful one. Mark a diagonal line across the square, then cut along this line so that you have two triangles.

Place one triangle on top of the other with right sides facing and two short edges matching; offset the edges by 1cm (3⁄8in) to provide for the seam allowance. Stitch them together and press the seam open. You now have a rhomboid shape.

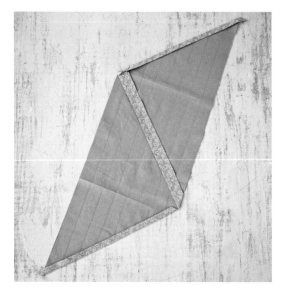

2 MARK THE BIAS STRIPS

Place the rhomboid wrong side up. Using your ruler, draw a line parallel to one of the longer diagonal edges, to the width required for your bias binding maker. Continue marking lines across the fabric. You may have a narrower strip left over; just trim this off. Mark identically spaced lines along the right side of the fabric. Along the shorter diagonal edges, press 1cm (³⁄₈in) to the wrong side; this will become the next seam allowance.

3 BRING THE SHORT EDGES TOGETHER

Place the fabric right side up. Bring the folded and pressed diagonal edges towards each other as shown. You will notice that the lines you marked on the fabric now line up vertically, forming columns.

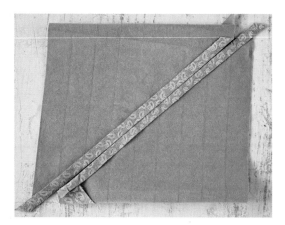

4 RE-ALIGN THE STRIPS

Next, move one pressed edge along by one column, as shown (this will ensure that you have a continuous spiral when the fabric is cut); make sure that the lines on the seam allowances match up.

5 JOIN THE NEW SEAM

Pin the pressed-back edges together (also hand-tack if you wish), and stitch them together along their pressed folds, so taking 1cm (⅜in) seam allowance. Press the seam open.

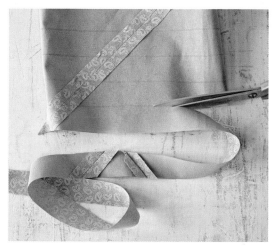

6 CUT THE SPIRAL

Cut along your marked lines; you will produce a long, continuous spiral of bias tape, which you can then use to make binding with a bias binding maker (see below).

USING A BIAS BINDING MAKER

Lay the bias strip on your ironing board, wrong side up. Feed one end of the tape through the wide end of the binding maker; you may need to give it a push with a small pair of scissors to get it started. With a hot iron, slowly move along your strip, pulling the binding maker and following it with the iron. This creases the side edges of the strip, producing bias binding that is ready to use. It's best to store the binding wrapped around something to help keep the pressed folds in place.

BINDING A NECKLINE OR ARMHOLE

Using bias binding at an armhole or neckline isn't just for decoration. It provides support and structure to help maintain the shape of the garment. The process is basically the same as for the 'Bound Hem' (see page 46), so you may wish to practise it first on a straight edge, as shown there.

Here is how I apply bias binding to get a really neat finish.

1 ATTACH THE FIRST EDGE OF THE BINDING

Start applying the bias binding at an inconspicuous place – at the side seam for an armhole or near the shoulder seam at the back for a neckline – leaving about 5cm (2in) free. Open out one of the binding's folded edges and line it up with the raw edge of the garment, right sides together; pin it in place all the way around, gently stretching it around the curves, until you get back to where you started. Again leaving 5cm (2in) of binding free, cut off the end.

Hand-tack if you wish, then stitch the binding in place, using the crease in the binding as a stitch guide and leaving a 3cm (1in) gap where the two ends meet.

2 JOIN THE ENDS

Lay the tails of the strip flat against the gap that's yet to be sewn, so that you can determine the exact point where the two ends should meet. Insert a pin into each tail to mark their joining point. Stitch the tape ends together at this point, first pushing the rest of the garment out of the way. Trim off the excess binding and press the seam open.

Finish stitching the binding to the raw edge across the gap.

3 ATTACH THE SECOND EDGE OF THE BINDING

◁ **Visible style** Using the tip of the iron, press the bias binding away from the main fabric all the way around the armhole or neckline. (It will help to use a sleeve board for this.) Now fold the binding in half over the raw edge and press it in place, making sure that the remaining creased edge of the binding covers the line of stitching inside. Hand-tack the binding in place. Now, working on the right side of the garment, topstitch the binding close to the seamline, moving slowly to ensure that the line of stitching stays on the binding.

◁ **Concealed style** Press the binding away from the main fabric as for the visible style. Then fold the binding again to the inside of the garment and press it in place. Now the bias binding and the seam allowances will be completely inside the garment. Hand-tack around the edge to secure all the layers. Working on the right side of the garment, topstitch the binding in place; use a guideline or other marker on your machine's needle plate to ensure that the stitching is a consistent distance from the folded edge.

PRACTISE THIS TECHNIQUE ON THE 'SIMPLE SLEEVELESS TOP' (PAGE 94).

ADDING YOUR OWN PIPING TO A SEAM

Adding piping to your sewing projects is also a lovely way to add detail and contrast. For example, inserting it in the seam joining a yoke and a bodice can break up a solid or strong-coloured fabric and accentuate the styling. Piping can also add depth and texture to accessories such as bags and cushion covers.

You can buy ready-made piping, but making your own from bias tape is really simple.

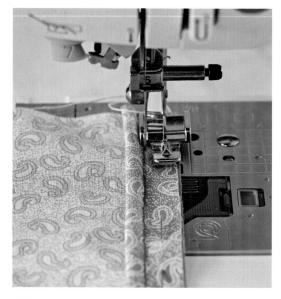

1 WRAP THE CORD

Make the required length of bias tape (see page 50), making it wide enough to go around the cord plus 3cm (1¼in) seam allowance, but don't crease it as for making binding. Fold the bias tape in half, pushing the piping cord into the fold, and insert a few pins as shown to hold it in place.

With the zip foot on your machine, stitch the bias tape around the piping cord. Work along the length of your piping slowly, ensuring that the tape is folded in half so that the raw edges are aligned. Don't worry about getting really close to the cord at this stage.

2 SEW THE PIPING TO ONE SECTION

Pin the piping to the right side of one section, with its seam allowances aligned with the edge. Using the zip foot, machine-stitch it in place. I use a long stitch for this – 4mm (⅛in) – as it's quicker and because this stitching is just to position the binding before it's secured in the seam.

PRACTISE THIS TECHNIQUE ON THE PIPED VERSION OF THE YOKE TOP (PAGE 180).

 JOIN THE SEAM

Place the other section on top, right side down, and pin it in place as for an ordinary seam. Again using the zip foot, stitch through all the layers, getting as close as you can to the piping cord.

 CHECK THE PIPED SEAM

Turn the work over and check that the piping fits snugly into the seam. If you can see some of the stitching from step 1 or step 2, just re-stitch the seam, trying to get a bit closer to the piping.

To take piping around a corner you need to clip its seam allowances so that they will spread out, as shown on the piped version of the Trimmed Cushion Cover (page 120).

Tucks, Pleats and Gathers

Along with the subtle ways of shaping a garment – by the cut and the use of darts – there are more noticeable, decorative ways: tucks, pleats and gathers. Of these, gathers are the easiest. They give a soft effect to the garment. Pleats and tucks, which involve folding the fabric and stitching it in place, give a crisper look. A certain amount of precision is required for those; but by taking each step in turn and making sure to prepare and mark the fabric accurately before you start sewing, you can achieve really beautiful results.

TUCKS

Tucks are folds that normally project out from the garment – or in some cases lie inside it – either vertically or horizontally. They can be stitched in place for the full length of the fold, making them purely a design feature, or they can be stitched only part-way down to give fullness. I love the neatness of them; there is something really satisfying about seeing a set of nice crisp, even tucks in a garment. See, for example, the tucks on my Apron variation, on page 144.

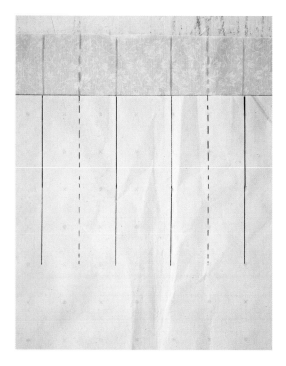

1 MARK THE TUCK LINES ON THE FABRIC

Tucks will be marked on your pattern piece by a series of lines. These can seem quite confusing at first glance, but once you look at them, you'll see that they make sense. The stitching lines will be marked with a solid line. Sometimes, but not always, the fold line will also be marked – typically with a dashed line. (The photograph shows tucks that will be stitched only part-way, to control fullness.) Transfer the marks to your fabric (see page 28). If your tucks are to be stitched in place for their entire length, first mark their positions at the fabric edges, then use a quilting ruler to help ensure that these lines are marked straight and evenly spaced. Use different-coloured chalk to mark the fold lines and the stitching lines to make sure you match up the right sets of lines.

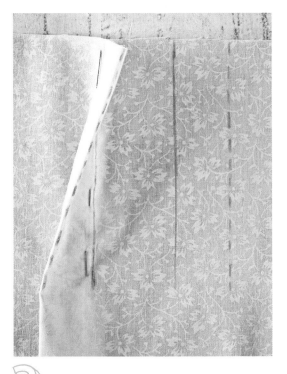

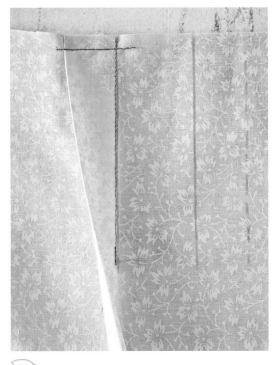

2 STITCH THE TUCKS

Work on one tuck at a time. Fold the fabric along the dashed fold line so that the two stitching lines are now matched up. (Your pattern will specify whether the right or wrong sides of the fabric should be facing.) Pin the tucks in place, checking that the stitching lines meet. Stitch the tuck, with a normal straight stitch, reversing at each end.

3 PRESS THE TUCK

Open the fabric out and press the tuck to the side. It will be specified in the pattern which side the tuck should be pressed to. You will usually then tack the tuck in place as shown, so that it will be correctly positioned for the adjacent seam.

Repeat the process for the other tucks marked on your fabric.

PLEATS

There are many different styles of pleat. Like tucks, they are essentially folds in the fabric, and they are often stitched in place for part of their length. Normally they are then pressed for the rest of their length, producing a crisp, structured effect.

A single pleat can be used to allow movement in a narrow skirt, for example; or a full skirt can be pleated around its entire width – as in a kilt.

The way in which a pleat is folded will produce different effects. A box pleat is formed by making two folds pointing away from the centre, as in the sample below left; whereas the inverted pleat, below right, has folds that point towards the centre. (On the wrong side of the fabric the positions of the folds in the two examples are reversed.)

Box pleat (left) and inverted pleat (right)

1 MARK THE FABRIC

There will be lines and a mark on the pattern showing where the line of stitching that holds the pleat in place should end (on the sample it's marked in yellow). Transfer the lines onto the right side of the fabric for a box pleat, or onto the wrong side for an inverted pleat.

2 STITCH THE PLEAT IN PLACE

Using the mark that indicates where the stitching line should end, sew the pleat in place, reversing at start and finish as usual. This stitching is done in blue on the sample. The remainder of the fold should be tacked in place, using the sewing machine. This tacking – here in red – will hold the pleat in place while you press it.

3 PRESS THE PLEAT

Press the pleat for its entire length (this is so that the fabric will hold its shape) then remove the tacking stitches.

GATHERS

1 ADD THE GATHERING STITCHES

Thread your machine with one colour in the needle and another in the bobbin.

This will make it easier to distinguish the two threads later. Pull out at least 15cm (6in) from both needle and bobbin, and set your stitch length at 4mm (6 or 7 stitches to the inch).

Sew two or three lines of stitching along the edge that you want to gather (do not fasten these). One line isn't enough – it will just break under the pressure – but over shorter distances, two may be enough. These lines must not touch or overlap, as this can cause the threads to break when you pull on them. Your pattern may specify where the lines should be, but normally one is positioned 1.5cm (⅝in) from the raw edge (or on another specified seamline) and the others about 5mm (¼in) to either side of it. Leave long tails of thread at the end of stitching, too.

2 PULL UP THE GATHERS

Separate the main and bobbin threads. Holding on to the bobbin threads only, push the fabric away from the thread tails to gather it up. Don't let too many gathers build up at one point, as it puts too much pressure on the threads and can lead to them breaking. It's a good idea also to pull from both ends, which will help to even out the gathers. Keep pushing the gathers along the thread until the gathered edge is approximately the same length as the section to which it will be sewn.

Pin the gathered section to the straight section at the key points (side seams and notches, for example), then distribute the gathers evenly. Add more pins, tack if you wish, then stitch the seam. Normally you will stitch along the centre line of gathering, so that the gathers themselves do not get caught in the seam, then pull out the exposed gathering stitches.

Setting in a Sleeve

Perhaps the commonest type of sleeve used in garments is the set-in sleeve. As its name suggests, this kind of sleeve consists of a separate piece of fabric, which is inserted into the bodice of the garment. Setting in a sleeve is tricky to get right because the sleeve is usually slightly larger than the armhole, so that there is some fabric manipulation to be done.

These instructions start at the point where the bodice of the garment has already been constructed, so that the side and shoulder seams have been completed. All pattern markings should have been transferred from the pattern to both pieces.

1 PREPARE THE SLEEVE

Machine-stitch three lines of gathering stitches between the notches as described for 'Gathers' (see page 61). The photograph shows the wrong side of the sleeve. Next, join the sleeve seam. Finish off its raw edges and press the seam open.

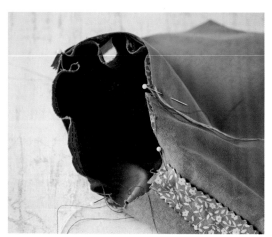

2 INSERT THE SLEEVE INTO THE ARMHOLE

Turn the bodice wrong side out and turn the sleeve right side out. Put the sleeve into the bodice armhole; their right sides will be facing.

Now pin the sleeve into the armhole, matching their corresponding markings. Match the bodice side seam with the sleeve seam; match the notches on the sleeve with those on the bodice; and match the mark at the centre of the sleeve head with the shoulder seam. It is normal for the sleeve head to seem a little too big for the armhole at this stage.

3 EASING THE FULLNESS

Holding the sleeve and bodice at the shoulder point, gently pull on the bobbin gathering threads (here the yellow threads) until the sleeve head fits the armhole on one side; repeat on the other side of the armhole. For most styles of sleeve very little gathering will be needed; on a puff sleeve, of course, there will be quite a lot.

4 STITCHING THE ARMHOLE SEAM

Even out the gathers so that the sleeve head sits flat within the armhole, with the raw edges aligned. Pin, then (if you wish) hand-tack the sleeve in place. With the sleeve uppermost as shown, stitch all the way around, 1.5cm (⁵⁄₈in) from the edge (or at the seamline specified by your pattern), starting at the bodice side seam. Move around the curves slowly, flattening out the fabric as you go, so that no puckers or tucks are caught in the stitching.

5 FINISH AND PRESS THE SEAM

Remove all the tacking stitches. Finish off the seam allowances together in your preferred way (see page 34), trimming them if necessary. Using a sleeve board, press the seam allowance towards the sleeve.

> PRACTISE
> SETTING IN A
> SLEEVE ON THE
> 'HAVE IT YOUR
> WAY DRESS'
> (PAGE 200).

The Projects

Beginners
Easy Peasy

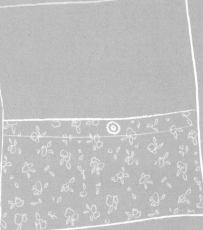

ENVELOPE CUSHION COVER
with Topstitched Border

This is the perfect first project for beginners getting to grips with sewing and using a machine, while making something really stylish for your home. All the basics and principles can be practised – from using a pattern and cutting out, to stitching seams and finishing them off neatly. The cushion cover has a simple construction and is all stitched together with straight lines, but the small added details, such as the topstitched border, make it look extra special.

Finished Size
50 x 50cm (20 x 20in)

Materials

FOR MAIN VERSION
60cm (¾yd) of fabric 140cm (55in) wide, such as lightweight cotton furnishing fabric

Coordinating thread

Dressmakers' pattern paper

Cushion pad 50 x 50cm (20 x 20in)

FOR VARIATION
Materials as for main version except: Cushion pad approx. 42 x 42cm (17 x 17in)

For Practising
STITCHING STRAIGHT SEAMS, P.30

FINISHING OFF SEAMS, P.34

HEMMING, P.44

TOPSTITCHING, P.219

1 CUT OUT YOUR FABRIC

Draw a 53cm (21in) square for the front of the cover and a rectangle measuring 53 x 38cm (21 x 15in) on your pattern paper. Pin these pattern pieces onto the fabric, making sure that they are parallel to the selvedge. Cut out the exact shape of your pattern pieces, cutting one square for the front and two rectangles for the back.

2 HEM THE CENTRE EDGES OF THE BACK PANELS

Lay the back panels out side by side, wrong side up, with two longer edges across from each other. These two edges will overlap on the centre-back of the cover.

Fold 1cm (³⁄₈in) to the wrong side along both of these edges; press. Fold again by the same amount and press, which will hide the raw edges.

Turn each rectangle right side up. Pin the folded edge in place, then stitch just under 1cm (³⁄₈in) away from the edge to secure this hem. As a reference point, align the folded edge with the right-hand side of the foot on your machine to help keep the line straight.

Lauren's Tip

IF YOUR FABRIC HAS A DIRECTIONAL DESIGN, LIKE THIS ONE, MAKE SURE YOU ORIENT ALL THE FABRIC PIECES THE SAME WAY, SO THAT YOU DON'T END UP WITH ANY UPSIDE-DOWN SECTIONS ON YOUR CUSHION COVER.

3 LAY THE FRONT AND BACK PANELS TOGETHER

Lay the front of the cushion cover flat with the right side of the fabric upwards. Lay one of the back panels on top, lining up the raw edges, with the wrong side facing upwards.

Lay the other back panel on top, again with the wrong side up and the raw edges aligned. Note how the back panels overlap in the middle. This will provide a neat gap, through which you can insert your cushion pad.

4 STITCH PANELS TOGETHER

Pin all these layers together, tack if you wish, and then sew all the way around the square taking a normal 1.5cm (⁵⁄₈in) seam allowance. Sew in one continuous line pivoting at each corner (see page 32) until you reach the starting point.

5 FINISH OFF RAW EDGES

Finish the raw edges using your preferred method (see page 34).

To get nice pointy corners, put your index finger into one of the corner points. Use your other hand to fold the seam allowance along the line of straight stitching. Fold the other seam allowance along the line of straight stitching so you have a little stack of folded fabric in the corner, as shown. Using your thumb and index finger, pinch this stack of folded fabric from the inside and keep a tight grip on it while you turn the cover right out for a lovely sharp, supported corner.

Repeat for the other three corners, then press the edges flat.

Lauren's Tip

TO GET A CRISP PRESSED EDGE, ROLL THE FABRIC BETWEEN YOUR THUMB AND INDEX FINGER UNTIL YOU SEE THE LINE OF STITCHING APPEAR. PRESS AS YOU GO ALONG TO MAKE SURE THE LINE OF STITCHING COMES RIGHT TO THE EDGE.

6 TOPSTITCH THE EDGES

Stitch about 3mm (⅛in) from the pressed edge of the cover, pivoting at the corners as you did before. This step isn't essential to the integrity of the cover but it adds a nice detailed touch.

Slip your cushion pad into the opening, and you are all finished!

✳ *Variation* CUSHION COVER WITH BORDER

Make the cover as for the main version, Steps 1–5.

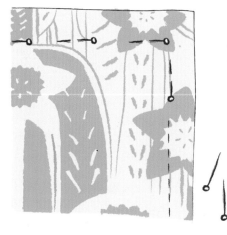

◁ CREATE THE BORDER

With the cover turned right side out, pin the front and back together, making sure they lie flat against each other.

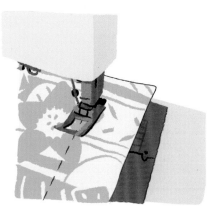

STITCH THE BORDER ▷

Using the marked lines on your machine plate (or a strip of masking tape), as a guide, stitch all the way around the cover, 4cm (1½in) from the edge, pivoting at the corners as before.

💡 *Other Cushion Ideas*

✳ Alter the size of the square, or make a rectangular version to suit the space that you need the cushion for. To work out how much fabric you'll need, measure your cushion pad and add 1.5cm (⅝in) seam allowance to every edge.

✳ Add buttons or hand embroidery to the cushion cover front to embellish it.

✳ To fasten the envelope and make it a feature, sew a few buttonholes (see page 41) along the overlapping back panel. Sew on buttons opposite the buttonholes.

SIMPLE TOTE BAG
For All Those Extras

Sometimes I find that my handbag just isn't big enough to carry all my extra papers and other bits and bobs, so that's when a tote bag comes in handy. And there is no reason why it shouldn't look pretty, too. The simple design of this one, with its contrasting front pocket, makes it perfect for showing off a favourite fabric. It's also a great first project on which to practise sewing straight seams. You can vary the bag by dividing the pocket into two sections, as shown on page 78, and trim the straps with braid. You can also attach the straps either inside or on top of the bag.

Finished Size
Approx. 40 x 37cm (16 x 14½in)

Materials

FOR MAIN VERSION:

60cm (¾yd) of main fabric (any width), such as linen, cotton-linen mix, cotton canvas, lightweight upholstery fabric

30cm (⅜yd) of contrasting fabric (as above) for pocket

Strip of interfacing 40 x 5cm (16 x 2in)

Coordinating thread

Dressmakers' pattern paper

1 x 2.5cm (1in) button

FOR VARIATION

Materials as for main version, except:

2 x 2.5cm (1in) buttons

FOR EITHER VERSION

1.5m (1¾yd) rickrack or other trimming

3m (3¼yd) of 18mm (¾in) bias binding

1 CUT OUT FABRIC AND TRANSFER MARKINGS

Draw a rectangle measuring 46 x 40cm (18 x 16in) for front and back, one measuring 40 x 25cm (16 x 10in) for the pocket, and one measuring 55 x 10cm (21½ x 4in) for the straps, onto your pattern paper. Pin these pieces onto your fabric and cut two of the larger rectangles, one rectangle for the pocket and two for the straps.

For Practising
ADDING A POCKET
SEE ALSO:
SEWING EVEN SEAMS, P.30
MAKING A BUTTONHOLE, P.41
TOPSTITCHING, P.219

2 PREPARE THE POCKET

Iron the strip of interfacing to the top edge of the pocket, following the manufacturer's instructions, then fold the top edge of the pocket 1cm (3/8in) to the wrong side; press. Then fold down another 4cm (1½in); press. Turn the pocket right side up and topstitch the flap in place 3.5cm (1⅜in) from the upper edge. This hides all the raw edges at the top of the pocket.

3 MAKE THE BUTTONHOLE

Using the buttonhole foot on your sewing machine, stitch a buttonhole (see page 41) horizontally in the centre of the pocket, about halfway between the upper edge and the topstitching.

4 TACK POCKET IN PLACE

Lay the front section of the bag right side up, then lay the pocket, also right side up, on top, with the bottom and side edges aligned. Pin and then tack in place along these edges by hand or with a long machine stitch, 1cm (3/8in) from the raw edges.

Sew a button to the front section underneath the buttonhole.

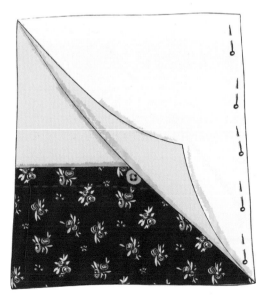

5 SEW BAG TOGETHER

Place the front of your bag right side up and place the back, right side down, on top of it. Pin them together (also tack if you wish); then, starting at the upper right-hand corner, stitch the side and bottom edges together, taking a 1.5cm (5/8in) seam allowance and pivoting at the corners. Make sure to reverse-stitch at the starting and finishing points.

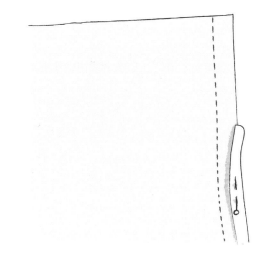

6 FINISH OFF SEAM ALLOWANCES

Finish off the seam allowances together either using zigzag stitch or binding the raw edges (see page 34). This will make the bag more robust, so that it will last longer.

If you choose to bind the seams, start the binding 7cm (2¾in) down from the top edge. Leaving that section unbound will help to reduce bulk at the top of the bag.

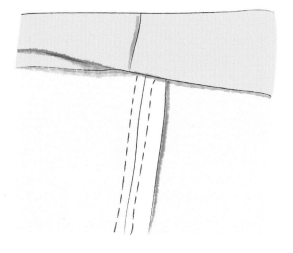

7 HEM TOP EDGE OF BAG

Press the side seam allowances towards one side. Fold and press 1cm (⅜in) to the wrong side along the top edge of the bag. (It helps to put the bag over the end of the ironing board when doing this.) Turn under and press another 4cm (1½in).

Turn the bag right side out and topstitch this fold in place 3.5cm (1⅜in) from the upper edge.

8 MAKE THE STRAPS

Fold each strap in half lengthways, with right sides facing; press. (At this point you can apply optional trimming, as described for the two-pocket variation on page 78.) Sew along the two short ends and long raw edges taking 1.5cm (⅝in) seam allowance, leaving a 5cm (2in) gap in the long edge.

Turn the strap right side out using a knitting needle or a chopstick. Turn in the raw edges along the gap and press the whole strap flat. Hand-stitch this opening using ladder stitch (see page 23) and press the strap.

Lauren's Tip

FOR A NICE CRISP EDGE, ROLL THE STRIP BETWEEN YOUR THUMB AND FINGERS TO BRING THE STITCHING TO THE SURFACE.

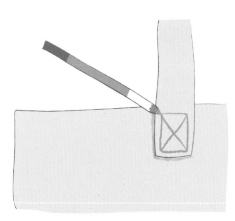

⑨ ATTACH STRAPS TO BAG

At each end of each strap, using chalk pencil, draw a rectangle 3cm (1¼in) tall and slightly narrower than the strip. Mark an 'X' inside this. Measure 10cm (4in) from the side of the bag and line the edge of the strap up with this point, positioning the bottom of the strap along the line of topstitching. Pin it in place. Stitch over the marked lines: first the rectangle, then the X. Do not reverse-stitch, but fasten the threads on the wrong side with a couple of backstitches (see page 23).

If you prefer to hide the ends of the strap, pin them to the underside and stitch them in place as above, working from the wrong side of the bag.

✳ *Variation* BAG WITH TWO POCKETS

MAKE BUTTONHOLES AND POCKET ▷

For Step 3 of main version, stitch two buttonholes, instead of one, placing their outer ends 8cm (3in) from the side edges of the pocket.

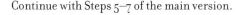

Fold the pocket in half vertically, wrong sides together; press the fold lightly. Hand-tack the pocket to the bag front section as described for Step 4 of main version. Now machine-stitch along the crease, starting at the bottom. When you reach the line of topstitching, sew a little triangle, as shown, pivoting the fabric at each corner (see page 32); then sew back down the same line to the end. This triangle reinforces the pocket.

Continue with Steps 5–7 of the main version.

◁ ADD OPTIONAL STRAP TRIMMING

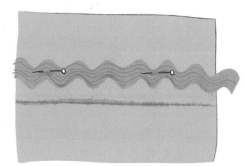

Fold each strap in half, lengthways, right sides facing: press. Place the trimming about 1cm (³⁄₈in) from the fold (it doesn't matter which side) and pin it in place. The distance from the fold can vary, but avoid placing it within the 1.5cm (⁵⁄₈in) seam allowance. Topstitch the trimming in place.

Complete the bag as for the main version.

SIMPLE BELT
With Mini-Bow

I love adding contrast when sewing, whether it is a panel of different fabric, a contrasting binding on an edge or a strip of braid. This belt, with its cute mini-bow, could serve to break up a busy pattern on a top or add some detail to a plain one. You could also vary the design by layering a trim over it (see page 84). The bow itself is so pretty you could make one on its own to use on a hair clip or a brooch, or you could sew one to a top as a style detail.

Materials

FOR MAIN VERSION

Strip of fabric 8cm (3in) wide and as long as your waist measurement (or wherever you want the belt to sit), plus an additional 45cm (18in). Suggested fabrics: medium-weight linen, twill, quilting cotton

Strip of iron-on interfacing 4cm (1½in) wide and the length of your fabric strip

2 hooks and eyes

Coordinating thread

FOR VARIATION

Materials as for main version plus ribbon/trim the same length as your fabric strip

1 button

For Practising

TOPSTITCHING, P.219

HAND SEWING, P.22

ATTACHING HOOKS AND EYES, P.43

LADDER STITCH, P.23

1 CUT OUT FABRIC AND ATTACH INTERFACING

First iron the fabric, then press the strip of interfacing to the wrong side, centring it, so that 2cm (¾in) of non-interfaced fabric extends to either side.

Lauren's Tip

WHEN YOU'RE TOPSTITCHING CLOSE TO THE EDGE THE FABRIC CAN SOMETIMES GET CAUGHT IN THE NEEDLE. YOU CAN PREVENT THIS BY USING A SHARP NEW NEEDLE AND BY GENTLY PULLING THE FABRIC FROM BEHIND TO CREATE A BIT OF TENSION IN IT.

2 PRESS BELT INTO SHAPE

Press the fabric strip in half lengthways with wrong sides facing. Open out and then press the raw edge in towards the centre fold on both sides of the strip.

3 FINISH OFF ONE END OF BELT

At one end of the strip, open out the folds and re-fold along the centre crease, placing right sides together. Stitch across the end through the interfaced section only, leaving the outer folds free. Remember to reverse-stitch to secure your stitching.

Trim the seam allowance close to the stitching. Trim the corners as shown to reduce bulk, then turn the belt right side out. Turn in the long raw edges and hand-tack them in place.

4 TOPSTITCH THE EDGES

Starting at the unfinished end of the belt, topstitch along one long side, across the finished end and along the remaining long side, 2–3mm (⅛in) from the edges; pivot the fabric at the corners (see page 32).

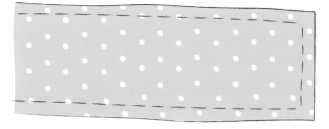

5 MAKE BOW LOOPS

From the unfinished end of the belt cut three strips, measuring 16cm (6¼in), 12cm (4¾in) and 8cm (3in), for the bow. Trim the remaining belt section to fit your waist comfortably.

Fold the 16cm (6¼in) strip so that its ends overlap slightly. Sew these in place by machine through all layers, as shown. Repeat with the 12cm (4¾in) strip. (The raw edges will be concealed later.)

6 COMPLETE THE BOW

Place the smaller loop section on top of the larger one with the raw, overlapped edges at the back. Secure these two sections together with a few hand stitches to keep them in place. Wrap the smallest strip around the loops to form the middle of the bow. You may have to trim this down a little so that the raw edges remain hidden.

Now slip the unfinished end of the belt into the underside of the wrapping strip. Hand-stitch these layers together with ladder stitch so that no stitching shows from the front of the belt.

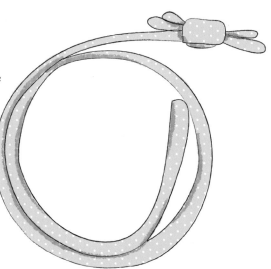

7 ATTACH HOOKS AND EYES

Sew two hooks onto the back of the bow and two eyes in corresponding places 1.5cm (⅝in) from the finished end of the belt. (Make sure to sew the eyes on the underside of the belt.)

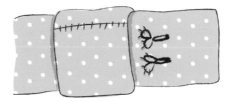 

✳ *Variation* BELT WITH LACE TRIM

ADD LACE TRIM ▷

If you want to add a ribbon or trim detail, you can do this after Step 2 of the main version. Open the pressed folds and lay the strip right side up. Pin the trim to one of the two middle sections as shown, then topstitch it in place and continue with Steps 3–7. Hand-sew the button to the centre of the bow as shown in the photograph.

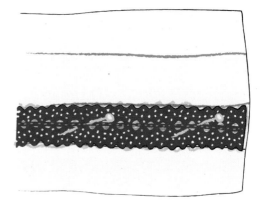

💡 *Other Variation Ideas*

✿ Embroider a pattern with a contrasting thread or even a simple running stitch with bright coloured thread. Do this on the the fabric before you stitch the belt together.

✿ Alter the width of the belt, just remember to allow at least an extra 1.5cm (⅝in) on each of the long sides of the strip to turn the fabric inwards to hide the raw edges.

Beginners
Moving On

✳ ✳ ✳ ✳

REVERSIBLE PLACEMATS WITH NAPKINS

Placemats are a really simple and effective way to make a table setting gorgeous, and making your own lets you use some pretty fabric to make something that can be used every day. Coordinating napkins make them even more special. Two placemat sets are shown here: classic placemats in opposing colourways with hand-embroidered napkins, and quirky placemats with cutlery pockets and rickrack-trimmed napkins.

For Practising

MITRING A CORNER

SEE ALSO
TOPSTITCHING, P.219
SEWING STRAIGHT SEAMS, P.30

Finished Size

Placemats, approx. 37 x 27cm (14½ x 10½in)
Napkins, approx. 39 x 39cm (15¼ x 15¼in)

Materials

FOR MAIN VERSION
FOR A SET OF FOUR PLACEMATS
60cm (¾yd) of each of two contrasting medium- to heavyweight fabrics, 110cm (43in) wide, such as cotton canvas or linen

70cm (⅞yd) of medium-weight iron-on interfacing, 90cm (36in) wide

Coordinating thread

FOR A SET OF FOUR NAPKINS
90cm (1yd) plain, medium-weight fabric (any width) for napkins

Coordinating thread

Embroidery thread, such as stranded cotton

FOR POCKET VERSION
60cm (¾yd) patterned fabric, 112cm (44in) wide, for placemats and pockets

1.5m (1¾yd) plain fabric, 112cm (44in) wide, for placemats, pockets and napkins

60cm (¾yd) medium-weight iron-on interfacing, 90cm (36in) wide

7m (7¾yd) rickrack

Coordinating thread

Placemats

1 CUT OUT FABRIC AND INTERFACING

For the placemats, cut four rectangles measuring 30 x 40cm (12 x 16in) in each of your two fabrics and four the same size from interfacing.

Iron the interfacing onto the wrong side of four of the placemat sections, following the manufacturer's instructions.

2 JOIN FRONT AND BACK OF PLACEMAT

Pin the front and back of each placemat together with right sides facing, using one of each colourway for each placemat. Stitch them together around the edges, leaving an 8cm (3in) gap in one side.

Cut diagonally across the corners to reduce bulk, then turn each placemat right side out. Tuck the opening edges inside, and press each placemat flat. Topstitch all the way around (which will close the gap), 3mm (⅛in) from the edge.

Napkins

1 PRESS THE HEM

Cut four pieces of your chosen fabric, each measuring 43 x 43cm (17 x 17in).
Fold, then press, 1cm (⅜in) to the wrong side on all four edges of each. Fold
and press another 1cm (⅜in), concealing the raw edges.

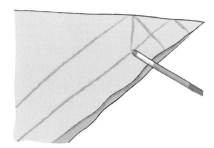

2 MARK MITRED CORNER

Open out the folds you just pressed, then fold the napkin
in half, right sides facing, to make a triangle. Pin the edges
together near one corner. At one corner, draw a short chalk line
at 90 degrees to the folded edge, from the inner crease to the
outer crease as shown.

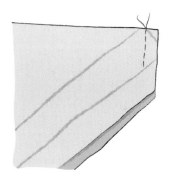

3 STITCH THE MITRE

Stitch along your chalk line, then trim off the excess fabric
at the corner. Repeat on the remaining three corners.
Press each seam flat.

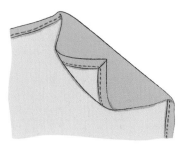

4 FINISH MITRE AND TOPSTITCH

Turn the stitched corners inside out, ensuring that you turn it all the
way to get a sharp point. You will now see your mitered corner.

Now tuck the raw edges under, as before, and press the hem flat.

Topstitch all the way around the edge just under 1cm (⅜in) from the
folded edge, pivoting at the corners.

5 DECORATE THE NAPKINS

Using embroidery thread and needle, decorate the edges of each napkin –
or just one corner, if you prefer – with your choice of embroidery stitches
(see photograph, page 88).

✿ *Variation* PLACEMAT SET WITH CUTLERY POCKETS

CUT OUT PIECES

From the patterned fabric cut the following pieces: four placemats (as for main version, Step 1) and two rectangles, for pockets, each 33 x 13cm (13 x 5in).

From the plain fabric cut four placemats, two pocket pieces and four napkins (as for main version, Step 1). Cut four placemat pieces from interfacing, and iron this onto two patterned and two plain placemat pieces.

◁ MAKE PATCH POCKETS

Fold each pocket section in half, right sides together. Stitch around the raw edges as shown, leaving a 5cm (2in) gap on one side. Trim the corners, turn the pocket inside out and press it flat, pushing the edges of the gap inside.

TOPSTITCH POCKET TO PLACEMAT ▷

Place each pocket in the bottom right-hand corner of a contrasting placemat, 5cm (2in) from the side edge and 3.5cm (1⅜in) from the bottom. Pin it in place, then topstitch down, starting in the top right-hand corner. This will also close up the gap in the side of the pocket.

COMPLETE THE PLACEMAT

Join the front and back of each placemat as for the main version, Step 2, using contrasting fabrics for each. Topstitch around the edges as for the main version.

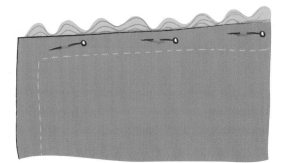

◁ MAKE THE NAPKINS

Hem the napkins, mitring the corners, as described for the main version. Pin the rickrack under the edge as shown and topstitch it in place, joining the ends neatly with a few hand stitches.

SIMPLE SLEEVELESS TOP
For a Summer Day

Easy to construct and fit but also versatile, this is the perfect project for stitchers making a garment for the first time. When I first started making clothes, it was a simple sleeveless top that boosted my confidence. I had a few really lovely cotton prints in my stash but was too scared to cut into them. I wanted a simple design that wouldn't spoil or compromise the print and would also let me wear and see the fabric more often. The tops I've made in a busy print fabric are perfectly complemented by something plain, such as a pair of chinos or a fitted skirt. This design would also look great in a plain fabric, worn under a cardigan or jacket.

Size

see page 208

Materials

FOR MAIN VERSION

80cm (⅞yd) of fabric 152cm (60in) wide, or 1.5m (1⅝yd) of fabric 114cm (45in) wide. Suggested fabrics: light- or medium-weight cotton, such as lawn, poplin, shirting, double gauze or voile

Coordinating thread

2m (2¼yd) of 2cm (¾in) bias binding

FOR VARIATION

60cm (¾yd) of main fabric 152cm (60in) wide, or 1.2m (1⅜yd) of fabric 114cm (45in) wide. Suggested fabrics: light- or medium-weight cotton, such as lawn, poplin, shirting, double gauze or voile

30cm (⅜yd) of contrast fabric, as above, 152cm (60in) wide, or 40cm (½yd) of fabric 114cm (45in) wide

Coordinating thread

2m (2¼yd) of 2cm (¾in) bias binding

1 CUT OUT PATTERN PIECES

Place the pattern pieces (see page 26) on your fabric, using the cutting layout (see page 209) as a guide, and transfer the markings onto the fabric.

For Practising

STAY STITCHING

SEE ALSO:

MAKING A DART, P.48

APPLYING BIAS BINDING, P.54

FINISHING OFF SEAMS, P.34

HEMMING, P.44

FRENCH SEAMS, P.35

2 STAY-STITCH NECKLINE

This line of stitching is worked on one layer of fabric at a time and will not be seen once the garment has been made. It prevents the neckline from stretching out of shape. Starting at one of the shoulder seams, stitch towards the centre of the front panel 1cm (³⁄₈in) from the raw edge. Repeat on the other side of the neckline. Repeat the stay stitching on the neckline of the back panel.

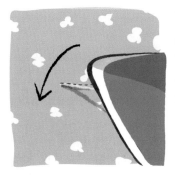

3 STITCH BUST DARTS

Using the pattern markings, stitch the front bust darts in place (see page 48); press them downwards. With the point of your iron, and using a circular motion, round out the point of the dart for a curved, smooth finish.

4 STITCH SHOULDER AND SIDE SEAMS

Pin the front and back shoulders together with right sides facing; tack if you wish and then stitch them together with a 1.5cm (⁵⁄₈in) seam allowance (to be used throughout the project). Press the seams open and finish them off in your preferred way (see page 34). Alternatively, join them with French seams (see page 35) to hide all the raw edges. This elegant method works best on lightweight fabrics.

Join the side seams in the same way, taking care to match the notches and keep the bust darts pointing downwards.

5 ADD BIAS BINDING TO NECKLINE, ARMHOLES AND HEM

The bias binding helps to maintain the shape of this garment and strengthen the neckline and armholes (see page 54 for full instructions). You can choose to have the binding showing, to add contrast and detail to the top, or fold it to the inside. Alternatively, you could combine both techniques to make a feature of the neckline but hide it at the armholes.

Fold the bottom edge of the garment 3cm (1¹⁄₈in) towards the wrong side and press the fold in place. Fold again by the same amount; press. Pin this folded edge in place (tack if you wish), then topstitch 2.5cm (1in) from the lower edge. Alternatively, for an invisible hem, hand-stitch (see page 45) or use the blind hem foot on your sewing machine.

 *Variation* TOP WITH CONTRASTING PANELS

CUT OUT PATTERN PIECES

Cut the two bodice pieces from the main fabric, following the line marked on the pattern piece for the variation. From contrasting fabric cut one front and one back panel for the bottom section, using the pattern pieces provided and following the layout.

ADD STAY STITCHING AND DARTS

Stay-stitch the bodice pieces at the neckline and make the darts in the front bodice piece as for Steps 2 and 3 of the main version.

◁ ATTACH CONTRASTING PANELS

Join the front and back panels to the lower edges of the corresponding bodice pieces, using a plain seam. Finish off the raw edges together (see page 34) and press them towards the bodice. Alternatively, use a French seam (see page 35), for a neat finish.

With the right side upwards, topstitch the seam allowances in place close to the seamline on the bodice, just above the contrast panel, on the front and back sections.

JOIN SHOULDER AND SIDE SEAMS ▷

The shoulder seams can be joined with a plain seam, as for the main version, Step 4, or, if you prefer, with a French seam.

Join the sides with a plain seam, stitching from the top downwards (first tack if you wish), matching the notches and making sure that the bust darts remain pressed downwards; stop when you reach the bottom panels. Remember to reverse-stitch to secure the seam.

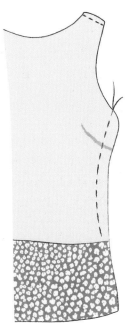

Lauren's Tip

IF YOU ARE MORE EXPERIENCED YOU COULD TRY A FLOATY SILK FABRIC, SUCH AS CRÊPE DE CHINE, OR A RAYON CHALLIS.

PRESS AND NEATEN SIDE EDGES ▷

Press the side seam allowances open, then turn the raw edges under again and press in place. On the bottom panel, press under 1cm (³⁄₈in), then another 1cm (³⁄₈in), so that the raw edge is concealed. Repeat along the bottom edge of the panels.

◁ MITRE THE CORNERS

Open out the folds you have just pressed and fold the fabric, right sides together, so that side and bottom raw edges line up and the inner crease lines meet at this new fold as shown. Machine-stitch from the inner to the outer crease, at a right angle to the folded edge (shown in pink).

Trim off the excess fabric outside this stitching. Turn the fabric right side out and tuck in the raw edges; you will see the neatly mitred corner. Repeat on the other three corners at the bottom of the top.

TACK SEAM ALLOWANCES AND HEMS ▷

Tack the folded seam allowance in place along the side seam of the bodice and continue tacking along the side and bottom hems of the front and back panels.

◁ TOPSTITCH SEAMLINES AND HEMS

Now topstitch along the seam and hem allowances 5mm (¹⁄₄in) away from the seamlines and hem edges. Work on the right side and start at the back bodice at the armhole. Continue into the bottom panel, pivoting the fabric when you get to the corner. Sew along the bottom panel and back up to the other side of the back panel to the other armhole. Repeat on the front bodice and panel.

ADD BIAS BINDING TO NECKLINE AND ARMHOLES

Bind the neckline and armholes as for Step 5 of the main version. In this variation it is concealed, but you could have it exposed if you prefer.

❋ ❋ ❋ ❋

MEMORY PATCHWORK QUILT

I'm happy to admit that I'm a complete fabric addict. I can't bear to throw any fabric away – from the smallest scrap of new material to old clothes with worn-out elbows and torn cuffs. I salvaged my husband's old cotton shirts to turn them into a quilt. So whenever we look at the quilt we have memories of shirts past!

You can use almost any type of fabric for this project – the variation on page 105 uses old outgrown baby clothes – and you can alter the size of the quilt by changing the size or number of squares.

Finished Size

For larger quilt: approx. 175 x 150cm (69 x 59in)
For cot quilt: approx. 100 x 90cm (39½ x 35½in)

Materials

FOR LARGER QUILT

A total of 2.6m (2⅞yd) of assorted patterned cotton fabrics, such as quilting cotton, 106–112cm (42–44in) wide, or the equivalent (for example, six or seven different shirts)

Piece of polyester or cotton wadding 2 x 1.7m (2¼ x 1¾yd)

3.4m (3¾yd) backing fabric, such as quilting cotton, at least 106cm (42in) wide

Coordinating thread

FOR COT QUILT

A total of 1m (1⅛yd) of assorted patterned cotton fabrics, such as quilting cotton, 106–112cm (42–44in) wide, or the equivalent (for example, ten or eleven baby grows)

Piece of polyester or cotton wadding 1.2 x 1.1m (1⅜ x 1¼yd)

1.2m (1⅜yd) backing fabric, such as quilting cotton, at least 106cm (42in) wide

1.5m (1¾yd) medium-weight non-woven iron-on interfacing (optional: if using baby grows or other stretchy fabric)

Coordinating thread

ADDITIONAL TOOLS (BOTH VERSIONS)

Rotary cutter, self-healing mat, quilting ruler, quilters' curved safety pins (optional), walking foot (optional), quarter-inch foot (optional)

For Practising

USING A ROTARY CUTTER
QUILTING BY MACHINE
MITRING A CORNER

SEE ALSO:
SEWING STRAIGHT SEAMS, P.30
LADDER STITCH, P.23

1 CUT OUT SQUARES

Using a rotary cutter, quilting ruler and self-healing mat, cut out 143 squares (or the required number), each 14 x 14cm (5½ x 5½in). Make sure you apply pressure to the quilting ruler to stop it from slipping while you are cutting, and always move the cutter away from yourself, keeping your fingers well away from the edge that you are cutting.

2 LAY OUT SQUARES

Find a large space to lay out all your squares. A double bed works well, or you can clear a space on the floor. It might take a while to arrange the prints to get a design that you really like. Take a picture of it, just in case things get mixed up. Label the rows A, B, C, D and so on, and keep them separate. (You can divide the squares into either lengthways or crossways rows.)

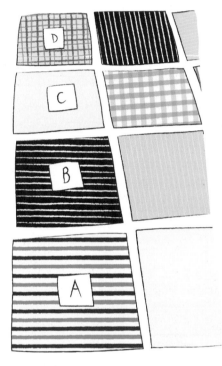

3 MAKE UP ROWS

Working with one row at a time, take the first two squares and place them together with right sides facing and edges matching. If the patterns are directional, be sure to line them up correctly. Stitch them together along one edge (the adjoining edges, according to your plan), taking a 5mm (¼in) seam allowance. (A quarter-inch foot will help you keep your seam allowances even.) Join the third square to the second in the same way. Repeat along the row to make one long strip of squares. Repeat for each row.

4 JOIN THE ROWS

Press the seam allowances to one side on each of the seams. For Row 1, press all seam allowances to the right, for Row 2, press all seam allowances to the left, and so on. This will reduce bulk where the rows are joined. Pin two rows together, right sides facing, matching up the seams that join the squares. Sew the rows together with a 5mm (¼in) seam allowance. Repeat for all the rows. Press all of these seam allowances to one side.

5 PREPARE QUILT BACKING

Cut your 3.4m (3¾yd) piece of backing fabric in half across the width to get two pieces approx. 170cm (68in) long by the width of the fabric. Seam these two pieces to get a piece twice the original width of your fabric; press the seam open. Trim this piece, leaving the seam in the centre, to get a piece 191 x 166cm (75 x 65½in); this is approx. 16cm (6in) larger in both directions than your quilt top. (Note that the seam will run crossways.)

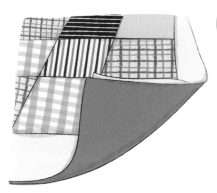

6 PREPARE QUILT LAYERS

Lay your quilt backing wrong side up and place the wadding on top. Then place your quilt top, right side up, on top of these layers, centred; the wadding and backing should extend about 10cm (4in) on each side. This excess will be used for binding the quilt; it also allows for any slipping of the fabric as you do the quilting.

Using long pins or quilters' curved safety pins, pin all three layers together with at least one pin in every square.

7 STITCH QUILT LAYERS TOGETHER

Stitch the layers together with the quilt top facing upwards, stitching directly over the seamlines. (Among quilters this is called 'stitch in the ditch'.) Start with a row in the middle of the quilt and work outwards to each side. Turn the quilt 90 degrees and stitch along the seamlines in the other direction. Continue until all the seams have been stitched. You will see a grid effect on the quilt back.

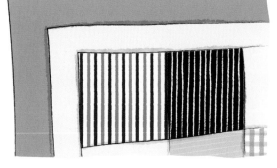

Lauren's Tip

WHEN STITCHING THE
MIDDLE ROWS, ROLL THE
QUILT UP TO HELP FIT IT
THROUGH THE SPACE
IN YOUR SEWING
MACHINE.

8 TRIM WADDING AND BACKING

Trim the wadding so that it is 3cm (1¼in) wider
than your quilt top. Then trim the backing fabric
so that it is 8cm (3in) wider than the quilt top.

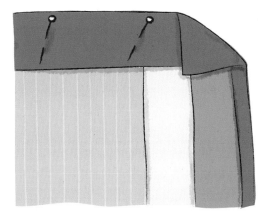

9 BIND THE QUILT

Fold and press 1cm (½in) of the backing fabric
towards the wrong side, then fold the backing fabric
over the wadding. It should overlap the quilt front
by about 1cm (½in). Pin the folded edge to the
quilt top.

10 MITRE THE CORNERS

When you get to a corner, fold it in as shown,
to make a triangle, then fold the next edge in as
before. Hand-tack the binding in place all around
the quilt. Sew the binding to the quilt top using
ladder stitch (see page 23).

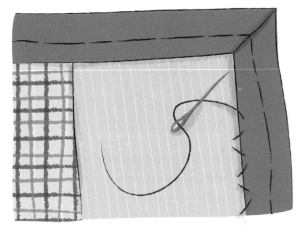

✳ *Variation* COT QUILT

If you are using baby grows or clothing made from stretchy fabric such as jersey, you will need to use iron-on interfacing to stabilize the fabric and take away the stretch before you cut it out.

If you are using baby grows, cut them open at the side and shoulder seams so that it lies flat. Cut out 56 squares of interfacing measuring about 15 x 15cm (6 x 6in) and iron these onto the wrong side,

following the manufacturer's instructions. Space them closely to use as much of the fabric as possible. Then cut out your 56 14cm (6in) squares, cutting through the fabric and interfacing, using a quilting ruler and rotary cutter on a self-healing mat.

Make the quilt as instructed for the main version. Because this quilt is narrower, though, you will not need to join pieces for the backing.

MEMORY PATCHWORK QUILT

QUILTED OVEN GLOVE
For Cool Cooks

An oven glove is an essential item in any kitchen. As it's something that you're likely to use most days, why not make a lovely one using some of your favourite fabrics? You can add detail by quilting a criss-cross pattern by machine; or, if you prefer, quilt a simple series of lines by hand (see page 110).

This project is also a good way to practise applying bias binding. Because you are applying it to a flat object, the technique is a bit easier than for a three-dimensional item such as a neckline or armhole. Even so, some dexterity is required, so once you've completed this project, you'll have the confidence to apply binding to garments.

For Practising

QUILTING BY HAND OR MACHINE

SEE ALSO:
STITCHING CURVES, P.32
APPLYING BIAS BINDING, P.54
LADDER STITCH, P.23

Finished Size

70 x 18cm (27½ x 7in)

Materials

FOR MAIN VERSION

50cm (⅝yd) of main fabric (any width) such as medium-weight linen, cotton-linen mix, lightweight furnishing fabric, quilting cotton

30cm (⅜yd) of contrast fabric, as above

50cm (⅝yd) of insulated wadding

30cm (⅜yd) of polyester wadding

Dressmakers' pattern paper and chalk pencil

2m (2¼yd) of 25mm (1in) bias binding, or a fat quarter to make your own binding (see page 50)

Coordinating thread

Walking foot

FOR VARIATION

Materials as for main version, plus:

Contrasting embroidery thread

1 CUT OUT FABRIC AND TRANSFER MARKINGS

For the main oblong glove cut four rectangles, each 80 x 25cm (31½ x 10in), as follows: two from the main fabric, one from insulated wadding and one from ordinary polyester wadding.

For the mitt pieces cut six pieces, each 25 x 25cm (10 x 10in), as follows: four from the contrast fabric and two from ordinary polyester wadding.

(Note that these pieces are somewhat larger than the finished pieces, in order to accommodate any movement or slipping of the fabric layers during the quilting.)

Using the pattern pieces, dressmakers' pattern paper and chalk, transfer the oblong shape onto the right side of the rectangular fabric pieces, but don't cut around it yet. Repeat to transfer the mitt shapes onto the square fabric pieces. On one of the oblong shapes and two of the mitt shapes, mark the stitch guides for the quilting, using a quilting ruler to help you get the lines parallel.

2 LAYER FABRIC AND WADDING

Place the unmarked oblong piece wrong side up and lay the insulated wadding piece on top of it with the shinier side down; place the ordinary wadding on top of that and finally place the marked oblong fabric piece on top. Pin all these layers together using long quilting pins or safety pins.

Repeat this process for the two small glove back sections, omitting the insulated wadding, which is not needed for the back of the glove.

3 WORK THE QUILTING

Attach the walking foot to your sewing machine and stitch through all the layers on all three pieces, following your marked stitching lines.

4 CUT OUT OVEN GLOVE SHAPES

Following the outlines you transferred in Step 1, cut out the oblong section and the two mitt sections. Hand-tack the layers together, about 1cm (³⁄₈in) from the edge.

Lauren's Tip

AS YOU ARE PINNING THE FIRST EDGE OF THE BINDING TO THE GLOVE, MAKE SURE TO STRETCH IT A LITTLE AROUND THE CURVES TO REDUCE BULK WHEN YOU COME TO SEW IT IN PLACE.

5 BIND THE MITT STRAIGHT EDGES

Along the straight edges of the mitt sections apply the bias binding as shown on page 54, but instead of topstitching the second edge of the binding, hand-stitch it to the underside of the mitt, using ladder stitch (see page 23).

6 ADD HANGING LOOP AND ASSEMBLE GLOVE

To make the hanging loop, first cut a 10cm (4in) strip of bias binding, then fold and press it in half lengthways with wrong sides facing. Turn in the raw edges to hide them and topstitch to secure them. Fold the strip in half and pin it in the centre of one of the oblong sections as shown. Hand-tack it in place with a few stitches.

Place the oblong section flat and lay the mitt sections on top, with the ladder-stitched side of the binding underneath. Pin them together around the edges.

QUILTED OVEN GLOVE

7 ATTACH BINDING TO RAW EDGES OF GLOVE

Attach the bias binding around the outer edge of the glove, mitt sections on top, catching in the hanging loop and joining the binding ends as shown on page 54.

8 HAND-STITCH BINDING TO UNDERSIDE

Fold the binding over to the underside of the glove and hand-stitch in place with ladder stitch (instead of topstitching as usual), ensuring that you fold it over far enough to cover the line of machine stitching.

Variation HAND-QUILTED OVEN GLOVE

▽ TRANSFER YOUR MARKINGS

Cut out pieces and mark them as for Steps 1 and 2 of the main version. When transferring the pattern markings to the main fabric, draw parallel lines as shown, placing them 2.5cm (1in) apart. Layer the fabric and wadding pieces as described in Step 2 of the main version and hold them together with safety pins.

Lauren's Tip

TO MAKE A FEATURE OF THE STITCHING, USE A RANGE OF COORDINATING THREAD COLOURS ON A PLAIN BACKGROUND.

HAND-QUILT THE GLOVE ▷

Using a good, sharp embroidery needle and embroidery thread, such as stranded cotton, sew running stitches along your marked lines through all layers. The stitches and the spaces between them should be about 1cm (³⁄₈in) long.

Complete the oven glove as for Steps 4–8 of the machine-quilted version.

GIRL'S SUMMERTIME SET
Skirt and Top

This cute little skirt and top set is so versatile, you could make the skirt in a medium- to heavier-weight fabric for everyday wear or in a lighter, delicate fabric for a party. The top is fully lined, so you could layer a sheer or lacy fabric over a solid lining to dress it up if you like. The straps are made of rouleau, but you could substitute ribbon.

This simple project is also a great way to get a little girl involved in the sewing process and excited about making clothes. She could help to choose the colours or fabrics and perhaps add little details, such as the trim and patch pocket used for the variation on page 118.

Size
see page 208

Materials

FOR THE SKIRT

A rectangle of fabric double your child's waist measurement (width) and 8cm (3in) longer than the desired finished length (cut along the selvedge). Medium-weight cottons or needlecord would work well, but avoid very thick fabric, which would make the waistband bulky and uncomfortable. Note: If the rectangle needs to be wider than your chosen fabric, buy twice the length of fabric, cut two equal pieces across the width, and join them with a plain seam.

Matching or coordinating thread

Piece of 25mm (1in) elastic the same length as your childs' waist measurement plus 2cm (¾in)

FOR THE TOP

Up to 1.1m (1¼yd) of main fabric

1.6m (1¾yd) bias binding (or ribbon) for straps

Matching or coordinating thread

FOR THE SKIRT VARIATION

Materials as for the main version of the skirt, plus:

Trim or ribbon long enough to go around the unseamed skirt

Piece of fabric 20 x 40cm (8 x 15¾in) for pocket

FOR BOTH VERSIONS

Rouleau loop turner (optional)

For Practising

INSERTING ELASTIC
MAKING ROULEAU STRAPS
ATTACHING A PATCH POCKET
SEE ALSO:
TOPSTITCHING, P.219
HEMMING, P.44

Gathered Skirt

1 PRESS WAISTBAND AND HEM IN PLACE

Fold then press 1cm (½in) to the wrong side of the fabric on one long edge, then press under another 4cm (1½in). This will be the casing, which forms the waistband.

Fold then press 1cm (½in) then another 1cm (½in) again to the wrong side of the other long edge. This will be the hem.

Lauren's Tip

MARK THE DISTANCES WITH CHALK FIRST THEN USE THAT AS A PRESSING GUIDE TO GET THE FOLDS AT THE CORRECT INTERVALS.

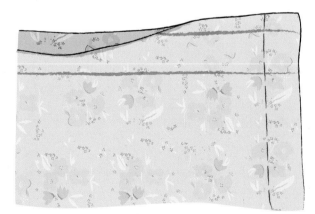

2 SEW THE SIDE SEAM

Open out the folds that you just pressed. Pin, then sew the shorter edges together, with right sides facing, to form the side seam. Press the seam allowances open, then finish them off. Alternatively, use a French seam (see page 35). You will now have a tube of fabric.

3 SEW WAISTBAND CASING IN PLACE

Re-fold the waistband along the pressed lines. Topstitch the fold in place just above its lower edge, leaving a 6cm (2½in) gap to feed the elastic through. Sew a second line of stitching around the very top of the skirt 3mm (⅛in) from the edge. This will help to stop the elastic from twisting.

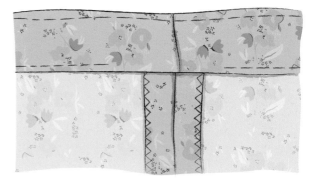

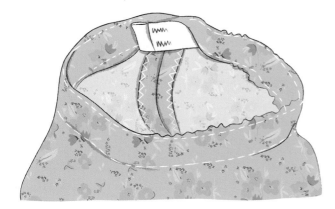

4 INSERT THE ELASTIC

Attach a safety pin to one end of the elastic. Feed it through the casing, taking care that the other end remains outside. When the first end emerges, overlap the two ends by 1.5cm (⅝in) and zigzag-stitch two lines to secure them. Now topstitch along the gap to close it, pulling the elastic taut as you stitch to stop the fabric from wrinkling up.

5 HEM THE SKIRT

There are lots of options here. You can simply topstitch the folded edge in place. Or you could add a length of ribbon or other trim and topstitch it while stitching the hem. Or you could finish the hem with bias binding, as shown on page 46.

Summer Top

1 CUT OUT FABRIC AND TRANSFER MARKINGS

Using the pattern pieces, cut two front bodice and two back bodice pieces following the cutting layout on page 210. Transfer all the pattern markings onto the fabric.

2 STITCH ROULEAU STRAPS

Cut four strips of bias binding, each approx. 40cm (16in) long. Fold the binding in half lengthways, right sides facing, and stitch a scant 4mm (scant ¼in) from the fold. This makes a very narrow channel (for a wider strap stitch 1cm [⅜in] from the fold). Trim the raw edges to 3mm (⅛in) from the line of stitching.

3 TURN ROULEAU RIGHT SIDE OUT

Push the loop turner through the channel until the hook comes out the other end. Use the hook to grip the edge of the fabric (this may take several attempts). Once the edge of the fabric is gripped securely, gently pull it through until the rouleau is turned right side out.

Tie a knot in one end of each strap to secure the raw edges and, if you made your straps a little wider, press them flat and top stitch close to the edges for a a really detailed touch.

4 TACK STRAPS TO BODICE

Following the pattern markings, pin, then tack the straps to the right side of one front and one back bodice piece, 1cm (⅜in) from the raw edge. This will be the lining.

5) SEW SIDE SEAMS

With right sides facing and notches matching, sew the front bodice lining to the back bodice lining at the side edges. Repeat for the outer bodice pieces.

6) JOIN OUTER BODICE AND LINING

Ensure that the straps are lying smoothly against the bodice lining, away from the top edge. Pin them in place, if necessary, so they don't get caught in the stitching. Place the lining inside the outer bodice so that their right sides are facing. Pin them together along their top edges, matching the side seams. Stitch all around. Clip the curves at the armholes.

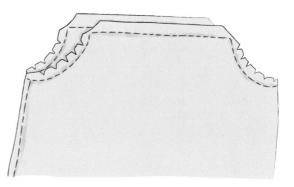

7) TOPSTITCH UPPER EDGE

Turn the top right side out. Press the seam flat along the upper edge, then topstitch 3mm (⅛in) away from it; this will help to hold the lining on the inside.

8) HEM THE TOP

Press under 1.5cm (⅝in) along the bottom edge of the lining; repeat on the outer bodice. Pin and hand-tack these two edges together (checking that they hang smoothly against each other), and topstitch them in place.

Try the top on your child and check the length of the straps. They should be long enough to tie a little bow at the shoulders; if they are too long, trim and re-knot the ends.

ADD TRIM TO SKIRT ▷

Once the waistband and lower edge have been folded and pressed, as in Step 1, pin the trim to the lower edge at your chosen position, measuring up along the folded edge at frequent intervals to make sure it is positioned evenly. Leave a little trim extending at each side of the fabric. Hand-tack, if you like, then topstitch the trim in place. Then sew the skirt as described in Step 2 of the main project.

◁ MAKE THE POCKET

Using the pattern on the pattern sheet, cut out two heart shapes for the pocket. (Or use another shape, if you prefer.) Sew the pocket pieces together with right sides facing, taking a 1.2cm (½in) seam allowance and leaving a gap of about 5cm (2in) in one straight edge. Notch the curved edges as shown and cut across the point close to the stitching, then trim the seam allowance to about 5mm (¼in). Turn the pocket right side out, then tuck in the edges along the gap; press the pocket flat.

SEW POCKET TO SKIRT ▷

Pin the pocket to the skirt in your chosen position and hand-tack it in place. Mark the top opening with pins (check your child's hand can fit in the gap), then topstitch the pocket in place 3mm (⅛in) from the edge, reverse-stitching at beginning and end to reinforce these points.

✳ ✳

TRIMMED CUSHION COVER

Because of their simple, flat construction, cushion covers are a great way to practise techniques such as inserting a zip closure and adding embellishments, such as the piping and lace trim used here. If your fabric has a bold pattern, it's best to keep the embellishment simple; a piped edge will give a neat finishing touch without detracting from the pattern. A plain fabric or one with a simple pattern, such as this stripe, can be a perfect base for more elaborate trimmings of various kinds.

You can make a sofa or armchair even more inviting and personal by adding cushions in your own style and colour scheme; and you can also vary the shape and size of the cushions to make them fit your space.

Finished Size

Both versions 50 x 30cm (20 x 12in)

Materials

PIPED EDGE VERSION

40cm (³⁄₈yd) of medium- to heavy-weight fabric at least 110cm (43in) wide (or 60cm [⁵⁄₈yd] if you wish the pattern, if any, to run horizontally)

Ordinary 23cm (9in) zip

50cm (⁵⁄₈yd) of fabric, any width, for making a length of 4cm (1¹⁄₂in) bias binding, or same length of purchased bias binding

2m (2¹⁄₄yd) of 5mm (¹⁄₄in) piping cord

Coordinating thread

FOR VARIATION WITH LACE TRIM

Fabric as for main version

Zip as for main version

70cm (³⁄₄yd) lace trim (or alternative such as pompom trim)

Coordinating thread

1 CUT OUT MAIN PIECES

For the cushion front cut one panel measuring 53 x 33cm (21 x 13in). For the back of the cushion cut two panels: one measuring 23 x 33cm (9 x 13in) and one measuring 33 x 33cm (13 x 13in).

2 MAKE THE PIPING

From the contrast fabric, cut and join enough bias strips, 4cm (1¹⁄₂in) wide to make a length of 2m (2¹⁄₄yd) (see page 50). Stitch this around the cord (see page 56) to make your piping. (Alternatively, you could use ready-made piping.)

For Practising

INSERTING A TRIM

SEE ALSO
MAKING PIPING, P.56
INSERTING A ZIP, P.36

3 PIN PIPING TO FRONT OF COVER

Place the front panel right side up. Starting along one of the straight edges (not the corner), align the raw edges of the piping with the raw edges of the front panel and pin in place; tack if you wish. The ends should overlap by about 5cm (2in). When you reach a corner, clip the piping seam allowances nearly up to the piping. This will help it to stretch and ease around the corner. You may feel that the piping looks a bit loose in the corners; this is normal. When the cover is completed it will stretch to fit smoothly around the corners.

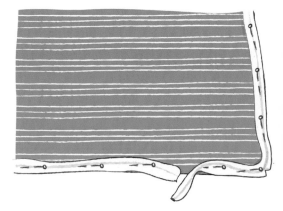

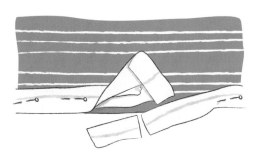

4 TRIM ENDS OF PIPING

Joining the piping ends can be a little tricky. First unpick the stitching on one end slightly to open it up, and then trim the bias strip to give it a straight edge. Fold under this edge by about 1cm (½in). Trim the cord so that it ends just short of the folded raw edge as shown.

Bring the other end close to the first end and cut straight through it so that it will exactly meet the cord on the other end.

5 JOIN ENDS OF PIPING

Slip the end you have just trimmed under the folded end of the bias binding, so that the piping will look continuous. Pin the joined ends to the edge of the fabric as shown.

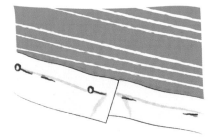

Using the zip foot and a long stitch, machine-tack the piping to the cover, removing the pins as you go. Don't get too close to the piping, as this might make the stitching visible once the cover is finished.

6 INSERT THE ZIP

Following the instructions for a standard insertion on page 36, insert the zip between the two back cover pieces. Position it halfway between their upper and lower edges.

You can position the wider of the two back sections either to the right or to the left. These are of different sizes just because the zip looks better off centre.

7 PIN FRONT AND BACK TOGETHER

First open the zip (you will need to turn the cover right side out through this opening). Pin the front and back sections together around all four edges; tack if you wish.

8 STITCH FRONT AND BACK TOGETHER

With the raw edges on your right-hand side, stitch the front and back panels together. Make sure that you get close to the piping cord. The zip foot may end up sitting slightly on top of the piping; this is all right, so long as the needle doesn't actually go through the cord.

Turn the cover right side out and check that you have sewn close enough to the piping cord to hide the machine tacking and the stitching you used to cover the cord. This is most likely to happen at the corners, as you can't do a straight pivot here as you normally would. If you can see the stitching on the piping, just re-stitch it, trying to get a bit closer.

Finish off the seam allowances together using your preferred method (see page 34).

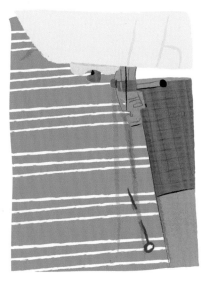

✳ *Variation* COVER WITH LACE TRIM

Cut the fabric pieces as for the main version, omitting the bias strips.

▽ POSITION THE TRIM

Cut two pieces of lace (or other trim) the length of the short sides of the front piece. Pin them to the fabric along the seamline on the right side. Bear in mind that 1.5cm (⅝in) of the fabric will be enclosed in the seam, so position your trim so that only the very edge of it will also be enclosed.

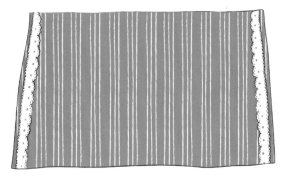

▽ FINISH OFF TRIM ENDS

At the top and bottom, fold the end of the lace back at an angle as shown, so that it will be hidden inside the seam. Tack the trim in place.

Make up the cover as described in Steps 7–9 of the main version, but using an ordinary foot to stitch the outer seam.

Improvers
Next Steps

✳ ✳ ✳ ✳

NECKERCHIEF
For a Dash of Style

I first started making these little neckerchiefs in order to use some of the lovely printed lawns that I had in my fabric stash, but without cutting into them too much. It's also a good way to use up leftover pieces of fabric. You can wear the scarf around your neck to add contrast to a plain top, or wrap it around your wrist as a sort of bracelet. The rolled hem makes the scarf fall beautifully and can be done either by machine or by hand. You can buy a special rolled-hem foot for most machines, but here I show you a simple method using an ordinary foot. A hand-rolled hem, used for the version on page 130, is a bit more work but produces a more rounded edge, with concealed stitches.

For Practising

STAY STITCHING
HAND-ROLLED HEM
MACHINE-ROLLED HEM

Finished Size
45 x 45cm (18 x 18in)

Materials
Piece of fabric at least 50 x 50cm (20 x 20in), such as cotton lawn or other lightweight cotton, or silk twill. Note: the piece should include the selvedge along one side.

Coordinating thread

Dressmakers' pattern paper (optional)

1 CUT OUT YOUR FABRIC

If your fabric is larger than 50 x 50cm (20 x 20in), cut a square of this size from dressmakers' pattern paper, then use this to cut out a square of fabric the same size; align one side of your pattern with the selvedge to ensure that you cut it on the straight grain.

Lauren's Tip

IF USING A SLIPPERY FABRIC, USE LOTS OF PINS TO HOLD THE PATTERN PIECE ON THE FABRIC. THIS WILL HELP YOU CUT ACCURATELY. OR TRY CUTTING WITH A ROTARY CUTTER.

2 STAY-STITCH EDGES

Using a normal stitch length, machine-stitch 1cm (⅜in) from the raw edge, all the way around the square. Known as stay stitching, this preliminary line of stitching will prevent the edges of the scarf from stretching out of shape as you stitch the hem. (This technique is also often used to prevent a curved edge from stretching before it is seamed.)

Trim the raw edge to 5mm (¼in) outside your stay stitching.

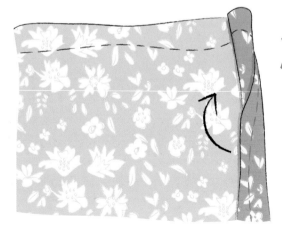

3 START FOLDING HEM

Place the scarf on a flat surface, wrong side up. Starting at the top right-hand corner, fold the adjacent right-hand edge to the wrong side just up to the line of the stay stitching, then fold again, to hide the raw edge. For the time being you will need to fold only the first 5cm (2in) or so of this edge.

4 STITCH THE HEM

Place the scarf on the machine and insert the needle into the double fold, about 2cm (¾in) away from the corner. (Because the fabric is quite fine and you will be working close to the edge, starting at the corner itself might cause the fabric to snarl up in the machine.) Holding the double fold in place, topstitch it down; continue to fold and roll it as you move along the edge. As you stitch, gently pull on the folded edge to create tension in the fabric; this will also help to prevent the fabric from getting bunched up and caught in the machine.

Stitch all the way down the first side of the scarf, right to the corner. Do not pivot the fabric as usual (the fabric will be too fine for this) and do not reverse-stitch. Cut the ending threads to about 2cm (¾in); these will be secured inside the corner when you secure the beginning threads in Step 5.

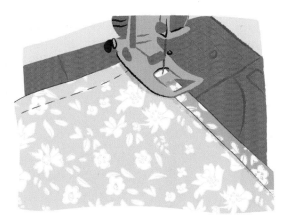

Now fold and stitch the next side of the scarf, starting at the corner where you just finished the last edge, in the same way as you did on the previous edge. Leave long thread tails for sewing in later.

Continue in this way, one side at a time, until you reach the starting point.

5 SECURE THE STITCHING

Thread each of the loose beginning threads into a hand-sewing needle and, using a backstitch (see page 23), hand sew the remaining sections of hem at each corner. Trim any stray ending threads (see Step 4) as close as possible.

❋ *Variation* HAND-ROLLED HEM

Cut out your fabric and stay-stitch the edges as for Steps 1 and 2 of the machine-rolled hem. You will need to work the stitching at your ironing board, or on a cushion on your lap, using a pin to anchor the hem while you stitch.

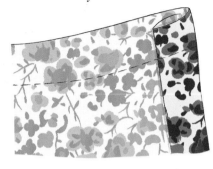

◁ START THE FOLD

Thread a sharp needle with one strand of thread and knot the end. Lay the scarf, wrong side up, on the ironing board. Starting at the upper right-hand corner, fold the raw edge to the wrong side of the fabric twice until the stay stitching is hidden. Insert a pin through the fold and into the ironing board.

MAKE THE FIRST STITCH ▷

Insert the needle into the fold and secure it with a little stitch. Work from right to left along the edge of the scarf, rolling the raw edge to hide the stay stitching. First, take the needle through the hem for 1cm (³⁄₈in) as shown.

◁ CONTINUE STITCHING

Pick up just a few threads of the main section just below the point where the thread emerges; this tiny stitch should be virtually invisible on the right side. Take another 1cm (³⁄₈in) stitch through the fold, just above the tiny stitch. Continue in this way all along the first edge of the scarf, pulling gently on the stay stitching to create tension to help you roll the raw edge. Move the pin along as needed to provide resistance and anchor the hem.

TURN THE CORNER ▷

When you get to the next corner, repeat Step 1, carefully folding down the raw edge to get the hem started, and put an extra couple of stitches in the corner to hold it in place. Anchor this corner with the pin to provide tension.

Repeat these steps until you are back to the starting point. Fasten the thread with a couple of neat backstitches.

This hem is supposed to have a rounded finish, so don't press it flat!

SNAP FRAME PURSE
Cash in Hand

I love making these little purses – especially for presents, as it is so easy to personalize them with a special fabric, with different pocket combinations, such as an extra pocket for cards, or by adding initials. Each purse is fully lined, and you can gather the fabric or make a little box pleat, which looks elegant in the leather variation on page 137. These purses are also a great way to use up scraps of fabric left over from bigger projects – you could have one to match every outfit!

Finished Size
14 x 10cm (5½ x 4in)

Materials
13 x 5cm (5 x 2in) snap frame

Piece of fabric 45 x 23cm (18 x 9in) such as medium-weight cotton or linen or lightweight furnishing fabric

Piece of fabric for lining 35 x 23cm (14 x 9in), preferably light- to medium-weight cotton

Piece of medium-weight iron-on interfacing 45 x 23cm (18 x 9in)

50cm (20in) of ribbon or other trim

1 button (optional)

Coordinating thread

Extra-strong glue suitable for fabric

1 CUT OUT FABRIC PIECES AND APPLY INTERFACING

Using the templates on pages 216 and 217, cut out the following pieces from the main fabric and interfacing: two lower purse sections and two upper purse sections. From the lining fabric cut out two lower purse and two upper purse sections and one pocket. Transfer the pattern markings to the fabric.

Apply the interfacing to the wrong side of the main fabric pieces following the manufacturer's instructions.

For Practising
INSERTING A LINING

ADDING DEPTH WITH A STITCHED CORNER

SEE ALSO:
GATHERS, P.61

PLEATS, P.60

2. GATHER THE LOWER PURSE SECTIONS

On each of the two outer, lower purse sections machine-tack two rows of gathering stitches between the two marked dots, 5mm and 1.5cm (¼ and ⅝in) from the top edge; leave long thread tails. Pull up the gathers to fit the lower edge of the upper piece, distribute them evenly and pin the gathered edge to the upper purse section, right sides together, matching the notches and side edges. Tack if you wish, then stitch with a 1.2cm (½in) seam allowance. Pull out the lower gathering stitches.

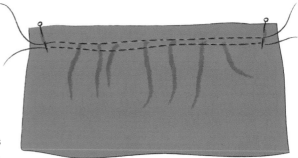

3. ADD THE TRIM

Before you sew the purse together you can add any decoration or embellishment you like. For the purse shown, topstitch or hand-stitch a length of ribbon over the seam joining the upper and lower sections on the front and back sections.

To make a little bow cut a 12cm (5in) strip of ribbon. Fold the edges in towards the centre and overlap them slightly; hold them together with a few hand stitches. Wrap a 5cm (2in) strip of ribbon around the centre of the bow and hand-stitch it in place.

4. ADD TAILS TO BOW

Cut two 5cm (2in) strips of ribbon and snip out a triangle from one end of each to minimize fraying. Hand-stitch these to one section of the purse (to be the front), then sew the bow on top to hide the raw ends. Add a button, if you like.

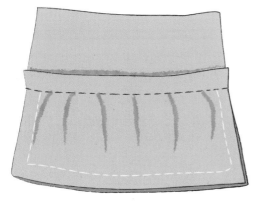

5 JOIN FRONT AND BACK OF PURSE

With right sides facing, pin (and tack) and stitch the front and back lower purse sections together, starting at the seam joining the upper and lower sections and taking a 1.2cm (½in) seam allowance. Don't forget to reverse-stitch for security.

6 ADD DEPTH TO PURSE

With the purse still wrong side out, use your fingers to press the seam allowances open at the side and bottom. Open the purse and fold it so that the side seam is touching the bottom seam. To ensure that the seams are aligned exactly, stick a pin though the middle of the side seam and check that it comes through the centre of the bottom seam; adjust it if necessary.

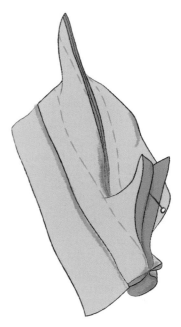

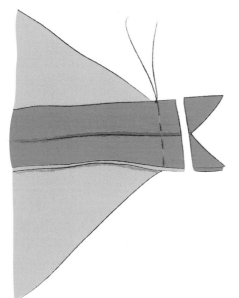

7 STITCH ACROSS CORNERS

Pin the seams together and then stitch across them as shown, from one folded edge to the other where the line will measure about 2cm (¾in), reversing back over this short seam to secure it. Trim off the excess fabric.

8 MAKE LINING AND POCKET

Join the top and bottom lining sections with a 1.2cm (½in) seam. Press the seam allowances towards the lower section and topstitch close to the seamline.

Fold the pocket section in half with right sides facing and stitch the side edges together, taking a 1.2cm (½in) seam allowance. Trim off the excess fabric and cut across the corners at the folded edge. Turn the pocket right side out and press it flat.

9 ATTACH POCKET AND COMPLETE LINING

Pin the pocket to one lining section, matching up the centre points and aligning the raw edges; pin in place. Topstitch close to the side and lower edges, remembering to reverse-stitch at the top corners.

Sew the lining together in the same way as you did for the outer purse in Step 5, but leave a 6cm (2½in) gap along the bottom edge for turning the purse right side out later.

10 PIN OUTER PURSE AND LINING TOGETHER

Match the top outer and lining sections of the purse with right sides together, placing the lining piece with the pocket against the outer piece with the bow, and pin them in place.

11 MARK FRAME OUTLINE

Place the purse frame over one side of the lining and draw around its outside edge to act as a stitch guide.

12 JOIN UPPER PURSE AND LINING

Stitch the lining and outer purse sections together along the marked line. Trim the seam allowances to 5mm (¼in) and notch the corners to reduce bulk.

Turn the purse right side out through the gap in the bottom of the lining. It may take a bit of fiddling around to get the two layers correctly positioned against each other. And you may want to press the seams flat along the top edges.

Lauren's Tip

USE PAPER CLIPS INSTEAD OF PINS WHEN PREPARING LEATHER FOR STITCHING, AS PINS WOULD BE VERY HARD TO INSERT AND WOULD ALSO SCAR THE LEATHER.

13 ATTACH PURSE TO FRAME

Apply only a small amount of glue to the inside of the frame, then slip the edge of the purse into it. Glue only one straight edge of the frame at a time, holding it firmly with your fingers until the glue has set and the purse is securely fixed before moving on to the next section. If your fabric is on the thin side, you may need to insert string or cord into the frame to help hold the fabric in place.

✳ *Variation* LEATHER PURSE

Before cutting out the pieces as in Step 1 of the main version, cut a piece of interfacing slightly larger than the pattern pieces and iron it to the wrong side of the leather; draw around the templates with chalk, then cut out the pieces. (First interfacing and then cutting makes it easier to get a clean cut.) Cut the lining pieces as for the main version.

◁ FORM THE PLEATS

Instead of gathering the lower sections of the purse, fold pleats in the leather, following the markings on the template. The folds should point out to the side edges. Hold them in place with paper clips as shown.

STITCH THE PLEATS ▷

Machine-tack the pleats 5mm (¼in) from the upper edge on each lower purse section.

STYLISH COOK'S APRON

I love cooking and baking, but like many cooks I usually end up covered in whatever I'm making! So for us messy cooks an apron really is a necessity. But there's no reason why it should be merely functional. Make it funky and part of your outfit by choosing a lovely fabric and adding little details, such as a contrasting waistband and ties attached with buttons.

This one has a full, gathered skirt with a plain bib, and I've trimmed the golden honeycomb fabric with a lovely floral print. The variation on page 144 is a bit more sophisticated, with contrasting striped fabrics (one with an Art Deco look), a straight skirt and a tucked bib – a great opportunity to practise this technique without having to deal with any complicated 3D construction.

Finished Length

85cm (33½in)

Materials

FOR MAIN VERSION

1m (1⅛yd) main fabric at least 110cm (43in) wide: medium- to heavyweight dress fabric or lightweight furnishing fabric

50cm (⅝yd) of contrast fabric, as above

2 large buttons

2m (2¼yd) of 2cm (¾in) bias binding

Coordinating thread

For Practising

APPLYING BIAS BINDING, P.54

GATHERS, P.61

TUCKS, P.58

TOPSTITCHING, P.219

HEMMING, P.44

FOR VARIATION

Materials as for main version

1 CUT FABRIC PIECES

From the main fabric cut the following pieces: skirt measuring 53 (tall) x 110cm (21 x 43in); bib measuring 25 (tall) x 38cm (10 x 15in); fold the bodice piece in half lengthways and pin the edges together. Using a ruler and chalk, mark a line from one outer corner to a point 4cm (1½in) in from the other outer corner. Cut along this line through both layers; you should now have a shape that is 38cm (15in) wide at the lower edge and 30cm (12in) wide at the upper edge.

From the contrast fabric cut the following pieces: two waistbands, each 68 x 8cm (27 x 3¼in); two bib borders, each 30 x 8cm (12 x 3¼in); one neck strap, 50 x 8cm (20 x 3¼in); and two ties, each 90 x 8cm (35 x 3¼in).

Mark the centre points of the waistband and one edge of the bib with a dot or a little snip in the seam allowance.

2 APPLY BIAS BINDING TO SKIRT

Use a saucer or other round object to mark the curved lower corners of the skirt. Trim off the corners.

Apply bias binding to the side and hem of the skirt (see page 46) so that the binding is visible on the right side.

3 ATTACH SKIRT TO WAISTBAND

Using the longest machine stitch, sew three lines of gathering along the upper edge of the apron, placing these 5mm, 1.5cm and 2cm (¼in, ⅝in and ¾in) from the raw edge; leave long thread tails at either end.

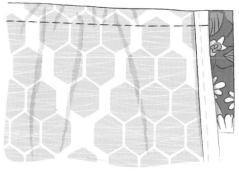

Set one of the waistband pieces aside; this will be the facing. Working with the other piece, pull up the gathers until the skirt is 3cm (1¼in) narrower than the waistband. Smooth out the gathers evenly, then pin and tack the skirt to the waistband, leaving 1.5cm (⅝in) of the waistband free at each end. Machine-stitch them together, then press the waistband away from the skirt. Pull out the lowest (visible) gathering stitches.

4 HEM BIB EDGES

On each side edge of the bib section, fold and press 1cm (⅜in) to the wrong side of the fabric, then fold and press another 1cm (⅜in) to enclose the raw edge. Topstitch the fold in place slightly less than 1cm (⅜in) from the edge.

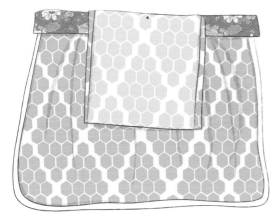

5 ATTACH BIB TO WAISTBAND

Place the wider, unhemmed edge of the bib and the free edge of the waistband together with right sides facing, matching their centre points. Pin and stitch them together with a 1.5cm (⅝in) seam allowance. Press the seam flat.

6 ATTACH WAISTBAND FACING

Position the bib over the waistband, so that their right sides are facing. Position the waistband facing, right side down, on top, with raw edges matching and the bib sandwiched between the two waistband pieces as shown. Pin them in place, tack if you wish, and stitch them together along the two short edges and the top edge.

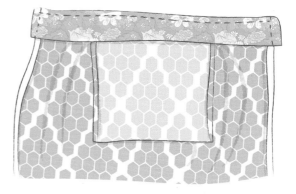

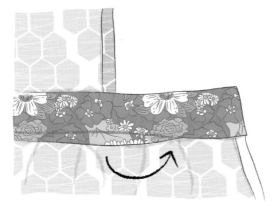

7 COMPLETE THE WAISTBAND

Cut diagonally across the waistband corners and turn the waistband right side out. Press flat. Fold under and press 1.5cm (⅝in) on the free edge of the facing to conceal the raw edges.

Finish by topstitching all the way around the waistband about 3mm (⅛in) from the edge.

8 MAKE NECK STRAP

Fold the strap in half lengthways with right sides facing and stitch the long edges together with a 1.5cm (⅝in) seam allowance. Turn the strap right side out and press it flat. Topstitch the two long edges 3mn (⅛in) from the edge.

9 ATTACH STRAP TO BIB BORDER

Pin and tack the neck strap to one long edge of the bib border, 2.5cm (1in) from the side edges.

10 ATTACH BORDER TO BIB

With right sides facing, pin and stitch the top edge of the bib to the bottom edge of the border. The ends of the border will extend 1.5cm (⅝in) to each side. Press the border away from the bib.

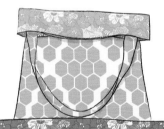

11 JOIN BORDER AND BORDER FACING

Sew the border to the border facing along the top long edge and short ends, enclosing the straps (using the same procedure as for the bib and waistband in Step 6). Cut diagonally across the corners, turn the border right side out and press flat.

 12 COMPLETE BORDER

Turn under the free edge of the border facing, as for the waistband facing in Step 7, and topstitch along all edges.

13 MAKE WAIST TIES

Fold each waist tie in half lengthways with right sides facing. Pin the edges together and stitch, leaving a 5cm (2in) gap in the long side. Cut diagonally across the corners. Turn inside out, using a loop turner or a blunt-pointed object such as a chopstick. Press the tie flat and topstitch all the way around close to the edge.

Lauren's Tip

DON'T FORGET, TO ENSURE YOU GET A CRISP PRESSED EDGE IT'S BEST TO ROLL THE FABRIC BETWEEN YOUR THUMB AND FINGERS TO BRING THE STITCHED EDGE TO THE SURFACE AS YOU PRESS THE EDGES.

14 ATTACH WAIST TIES

Overlap one end of the waist tie over the edge of the waistband and sew in place by attaching a button, stitching through all the fabric layers.

✳ *Variation* APRON WITH TUCKED BIB AND STRAIGHT SKIRT

From the main fabric cut a skirt measuring 53 x 65cm (21 x 26in). Using the pattern piece provided cut the bib, and transfer the tuck markings.

From the contrast fabric cut pieces as for the main version.

Bind the skirt edge and attach it to the waistband as for Steps 2 and 4 of the main version.

▽ STITCH TUCKS IN BIB

Ensure that you have transferred all the tuck markings onto the right side of the fabric. There are 6 tucks in total. Starting at one of the sides, fold and sew the innermost tuck first, sewing from the top of the bib section to the bottom. See page 58 for further guidance on this.

Continue to sew the remaining two tucks in place and press them all to the side.

Repeat with the tucks on the other side. Tack the tucks in place 1cm (³⁄₈in) from the top and bottom edges.

Complete the apron as described in Steps 5–14 of the main version.

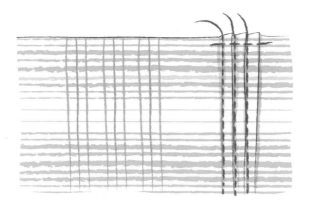

BIG WEEKEND BAG

I've never been known for travelling light, but I don't always want to sport a wheelie suitcase. That's why this simple bag is so roomy. The basic shape serves as a blank canvas for your own preferred features.

This bag has two external pockets plus a zippered pocket in the lining, magnetic snap fastener and an internal swivel hook for your keys. The machine-quilted variation on page 152 has two large internal pockets and a tab closing. Both bags have an ample gusset on the bottom, reinforced with extra-strong cardboard, and strong straps.

Finished Size

Approx 57cm wide x 41cm tall x 17cm deep (22½ x 16 x 6¾in)

Materials

FOR MAIN VERSION

1m (1⅛yd) of main fabric, at least 110cm (43in) wide, such as medium- to heavyweight cotton, cotton canvas, heavyweight linen, lightweight cotton furnishing fabric; you may need a bit more if your fabric has a large pattern repeat

1.5m (1¾yd) of contrast fabric, as above, for lining

2m (2¼yd) of non-woven iron-on medium- or heavyweight interfacing, at least 90cm (36in) wide

Coordinating thread

1m (1yd) cotton webbing for strap

1 large magnetic snap fastener

2 large rivet-type snap fasteners (see page 43), or sew-in fasteners

18cm (7in) zip

60cm (¾yd) rickrack or ribbon

Small swivel hook for keys

Coordinating thread

Piece of extra-thick strong card, 57 x 17cm (22½ x 6¾in)

FOR VARIATION

Main fabric, lining fabric, interfacing webbing, snap fasteners, card and thread as for main version

60cm (¾yd) of polyester wadding, at least 90cm (36in) wide

60cm (¾yd) of lightweight cotton such as lawn or muslin, at least 90cm (36in)wide

Walking foot

Quilting pins or safety pins

Contrasting stranded embroidery thread and embroidery needle (optional)

For Practising

ADDING A LINING

APPLYING INTERFACING

CREATING DEPTH WITH A GUSSET

SECURING A STRAP

QUILTING

SEE ALSO

WINDOW ZIP INSERTION, P.39

TOPSTITCHING, P.219

1 CUT OUT AND INTERFACE FABRIC PIECES

From the main fabric cut the following pieces:

· Two back/front panels: 60 x 45cm (23½ x 17¾in)
· Two side panels: 45 x 20cm (17¾ x 8in)
· One bottom panel: 60 x 20cm (23½ x 8in)

From the contrast lining fabric cut the following pieces:

· Two back/front panels: 60 x 45cm (23½ x 17¾in)
· Two side panels: 45 x 20cm (17¾ x 8in)
· One bottom panel: 60 x 20cm (23½ x 8in)
· Two side pocket pieces: 25 x 20cm (10 x 8in)
· Two hidden pocket pieces: 30 x 20cm (12 x 8in)

From the interfacing cut the following pieces:

· Two back/front panels: 60 x 45cm (23½ x 17¾in)
· Two side panels: 45 x 20cm (17¾ x 8in)
· One bottom panel: 60 x 20cm (23½ x 8in)
· Two side pocket pieces: 25 x 20cm (10 x 8in)
· One hidden pocket piece: 30 x 20cm (12 x 8in)

Apply the interfacing to the corresponding pieces of the main fabric, following the manufacturer's instructions.

Lauren's Tip

WHEN APPLYING THE INTERFACING, PRESS IT ON BIT BY BIT. TRY TO AVOID MOVING THE IRON BACK AND FORTH TOO MUCH, AS THIS CAN CAUSE THE INTERFACING TO MOVE OR RIPPLE.

2 HEM TOP OF POCKETS

Fold and press under 1.5cm (⅝in) along the top edge of each side pocket, then turn the edge under again by the same amount to conceal the raw edges. Pin and topstitch the hem in place 2mm (scant ⅛in) and 1cm (⅜in) from the top.

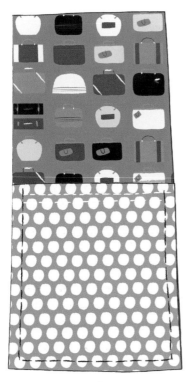

3 TACK POCKETS TO SIDE PANELS

Place each pocket, right side up, on the right side of a side panel, lining up the raw edges at the sides and bottom. Using a long stitch length, machine-tack the pocket in place, 1cm (⅜in) from the edge.

4 JOIN SIDE AND FRONT PANELS

Lay the front panel flat, right side up. Place the two side panels on top, right sides down, matching the raw edges. Pin and stitch them to the front panel, starting at the top but stopping 1.5cm (⅝in) from the bottom.

5 TOPSTITCH SIDE SEAMS

Open out the side panels and turn all the seam allowances towards the front panel. With right side up, topstitch along the front panel, 2mm (scant ⅛in) from the seamline (which will catch in the seam allowances), again stopping 1.5cm (⅝in) from the bottom edge.

Repeat Steps 4 and 5 to join the side panels to the back panel.

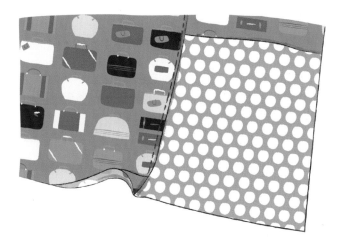

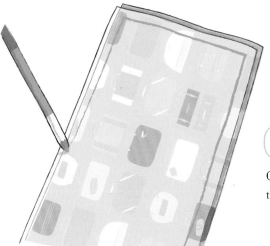

6 MARK STITCHING LINE ON BOTTOM PANEL

On the wrong side of the bottom panel, mark the stitching line 1.5cm (⅝in) from the edge.

7 ATTACH BOTTOM PANEL

Turn the bag wrong side out and pin the bottom panel to the bottom edge of the bag. As you stopped your side seams 1.5cm (⅝in) from the bottom edges, you will now be able to open these out in order to match up the raw edges to the bottom panel.

Stitch the bottom panel to the bag in four separate stages, following your marked stitching line.

Turn the seam allowances towards the front panel and topstitch down as in Step 5. It can be a little tricky to get right into the corners. Repeat along the bottom edge of the back panel.

8 MAKE HIDDEN POCKET IN LINING

Using the window placement guide given on page 39, mark the window opening for the zip on one of the larger (front/back) lining pieces, 12cm (4¾in) from the top edge and centred between the two side edges. Mark this also on one of the hidden pocket pieces, 3cm (1¼in) from the top edge and centred between the side edges. Iron the rectangle of interfacing over the markings to reinforce the opening. The chalk markings should still show through, but you may have to go over them to make them clearer.

Following the instructions on page 39 for a window zip, insert the zip in the main lining piece and the marked pocket piece.

Placing right sides together, pin and stitch the unmarked pocket piece to the one containing the zip around all four edges. Press the seam allowances flat.

9 MAKE THE KEY CHAIN

Thread the rickrack or ribbon through the loop on the swivel hook, then fold it in half. Pin the joined ends of the rickrack to a side edge (either side) of the lining panel containing the pocket 10cm (4in) from the top edge. Using zigzag stitch and working inside the seam allowance, stitch over the raw edges of the rickrack two or three times to attach them securely.

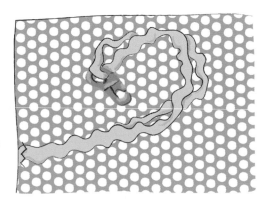

10 JOIN LINING SECTIONS

Join the front, back, side and bottom panels in the same way as for the outer bag, but omitting the topstitching and, instead, pressing the seam allowances open.

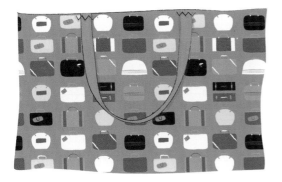

11 ATTACH THE HANDLES

Cut the length of cotton webbing in half. Pin each handle to the top of the front/back panel of the outer bag, 15cm (6in) from the side seams. Working within the seam allowance, zigzag-stitch the ends in place, stitching back and forth a few times to attach them securely.

12 INSERT THE LINING

Turn under and press 1.5cm (⅝in) along the top edge of both the outer bag and the lining. Place the lining (wrong side out) inside the outer bag (right side out). Pin the two layers together, matching up first the side seams then the centre of the front and back panels. Continue pinning along the rest of the top edge, making sure the raw edges stay turned inside.

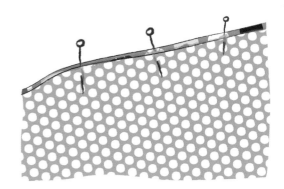

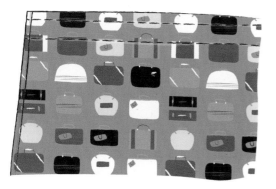

13 STITCH BAG AND LINING TOGETHER

Topstitch the outer bag and lining together 3mm (⅛in) and 1.2cm (½in) from the top edge.

14 ATTACH SNAP FASTENERS

Sew one half of the magnetic snap fastener to the top edge of the front and back panels at the centre of each, stitching through the lining and seam allowances only.

To help keep the top of the bag closed when it isn't completely full of stuff, attach the two rivet-type fasteners to the upper corners of the side panels as shown. (Or use sew-in fasteners, if you prefer.)

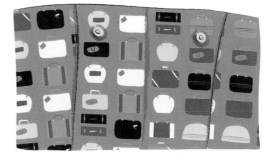

Variation QUILTED BAG

CUT OUT FABRIC PIECES

Cut out the pieces for the outer bag and lining as for the main version, but omitting the two side pockets and hidden pockets (including the interfacing for those). In addition, cut the following pieces:

From the main fabric cut one internal pocket panel, 65 x 30cm (25½ x 12in), and two closing tab pieces, 15 x 11cm (6 x 4¼in).

From wadding cut two pieces 70 x 55cm (27½ x 21½in) and one piece 17 x 14cm (6¾ x 5½in).

From muslin cut two pieces 70 x 55cm (27½ x 21½in).

Interface the outer bag pieces as for the main version.

Lauren's Tip

TO ENSURE YOU CUT OUT YOUR PANELS ON THE STRAIGHT GRAIN, MEASURE AND MARK YOUR FABRIC FROM THE SELVEDGE, OR CUT OUT YOUR OWN PATTERN PIECES FROM PATTERN PAPER AND PIN THEM TO YOUR FABRIC AS A GUIDE.

◁ MAKE AND ATTACH INTERNAL POCKET

Hem the pocket as for the side pockets in Step 2. Fold the pocket in half crossways and press the fold to mark the centre. Also mark the centre of one main lining piece. Pin the pocket to the side edges of the lining piece and machine-tack the edges together. (You will see that it is slightly too wide; this excess will be dealt with later.)

Align the creases on the pocket and lining and pin them together. Machine-stitch along the crease to divide the pocket into two sections. When you reach the top, stitch a little triangle as shown; this will reinforce the top of the pocket.

FORM PLEATS IN POCKETS ▷

At the bottom edge of each pocket section make a small fold in the centre; pin this in place. Machine-tack the bottom edges of pocket and lining together, 1cm (³⁄8in) from the edge, which will take in the little pleats also.

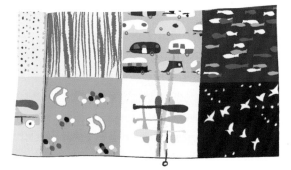

ASSEMBLE LAYERS FOR QUILTING ▷

Lay the muslin flat, place the wadding on top and place the front panel, right side up and centred, on top of that. (Some of the excess wadding and muslin will be drawn in during the quilting.) Pin the layers together with long quilting pins or safety pins; tack, if you wish, at intervals across the fabric.

◁ WORK THE QUILTING

Attach the walking foot to your sewing machine. This special foot will help to feed the fabric from the top as well as from the bottom. You can quilt along straight lines as shown or follow parts of the design of your fabric. Start sewing as close as you can to the centre of the panel and work your way outwards. If you are going to stitch a grid pattern, you can start at the centre of one of the edges and then work your way to right and left.

STITCH AND TRIM EDGES ▷

When you have finished the quilting, stitch around the panel, 1cm (³⁄₈in) from the edge. Finally trim the excess wadding and muslin from the edge of the panel.

Quilt the back panel in the same way.

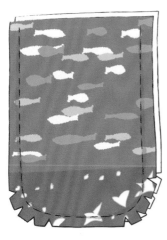

◁ MAKE AND ATTACH CLOSING TAB

Tack the wadding piece to the wrong side of one tab piece, then trim the wadding to size. Pin the other tab on top of the first one, right sides facing, tack if you wish, and stitch them together around one short and two long sides, curving slightly at the corners as shown. (You may wish first to mark this stitching line with chalk.) Trim the seam allowance to half its width and notch the corners.

Turn the tab right side out, press it flat and topstitch, 3mm (⅛in) from the seamed edge.

ATTACH TAB TO BAG ▷

Pin and tack the tab to the right side of the back panel, centred and aligned along the top edge.

ASSEMBLE BAG AND LINING

Following Steps 4–7 and 10–13 of main version, assemble the outer bag and lining. Attach the magnetic snap fastener to the underside of the closing tab and the right side of the bag front, 8cm (3in) from the top edge. If you wish, decorate the handles with lines of running stitch, worked in standard cotton thread, before sewing them in place.

Other Variation Ideas

❋ Try creating your own patchwork as described in the memory patchwork quilt project on page 101.

❋ Add a decorative running stitch along the sides of the straps.

LINED ROMAN BLIND

Making your own home furnishings can be really rewarding. You get to see your creations every day; and as well as looking lovely, they are so useful. Blinds are especially satisfying to make, and a lined Roman blind such as this one is both elegant and practical. In addition to the wealth of furnishing fabrics suitable for the blind, you have a choice of lots of lining fabrics, from the classic cotton and polycotton sateen to blackouts and fleecy thermal ones. This project will work with any type of lining, so you can choose what qualities you would like it to have.

You can also choose to add a bit of detail with a decorative trim along the bottom of the blind, as shown on page 163.

Materials

For quantities, see 'Measurements and Calculations' on page 158 or steps as indicated.

Main fabric: light- to medium-weight furnishing fabric works best, though if you choose a thicker lining fabric you could use a light cotton fabric for the blind itself. (If the blind's finished width is wider than your fabric, you will need to buy at least twice the length – more if a pattern needs to be matched – and seam it. Ask the sales assistant for advice.)

Lining fabric

Roman blind tape: this is like a tube, with small loops on it that you feed the blind cord through

Blind cord: this is a fine white cord, usually 2–3mm (⅛in) thick; for quantity, see Step 9

Hook and loop tape (Velcro)

Wooden or plastic dowel rods, cut to the required measurement, to fit in Roman blind tape channel

2 x 2cm (¾ x ¾in) wooden batten, which is secured to top of window frame

Flat wooden batten 2cm x 5mm (¾ x ¼in) to add weight to the blind

Staple gun or tacks and hammer

Screw eyes; for quantity see Step 9

Screws, rawl plugs and drill (see Step 9)

Blind pull: this is used to pull the blind up and down

Cleat: this is attached to the window frame to hold the blind cord

For Practising

CALCULATING QUANTITIES

SEE ALSO:
LADDER STITCH, P.23
TOPSTITCHING, P.219

MEASUREMENTS AND CALCULATIONS

Using some paper (preferably graph paper) and a ruler, pencil and a calculator, make a plan of your blind.

❀ Decide on the finished size of the blind; it can sit inside or outside the window frame.

❀ If your fabric has a large pattern, centre the pattern. For example, if there is a large flower motif, make sure that one of these will be equidistant from the two sides. Make a note of this distance to keep handy when cutting your fabric. Also make sure that there will be a complete flower at the top of the blind.

❀ The main fabric needs to be cut 7cm (2¾in) wider than the finished width of the blind and 6cm (2¼in) longer.

❀ The lining needs to be cut 1cm (½in) narrower and 6cm (2½in) longer than the finished blind width.

❀ The hook and loop tape should measure the same as the finished width of the blind.

❀ The top wooden batten should be the same length as the width of the finished blind.

❀ The bottom batten should be 2–3cm (approx. 1in) shorter than the finished width of the blind.

❀ For each fold in the blind you will need a strip of Roman blind tape that is 10cm (4in) longer than the finished width of the blind. It usually frays easily, so it's safer to have extra and trim it off later.

❀ For each fold in the blind you will need a dowel rod 5mm (¼in) in diameter that is 2–3cm (approx. 1in) shorter than the finished width of the blind.

❀ To work out how many folds you will have in the blind, decide on the approximate depth you would like the folds to be when the blind is pulled up. This is usually between 10cm (4in) and 15cm (6in) – so, a distance between strips of tape of 20–30cm (8–12in); but this will depend on the size of your window.

The following example is based on a blind measuring 117cm (45in) in length when finished.

↕ 13cm (5in)	
↕ 13cm (5in)	26cm (10in)
↕ 13cm (5in)	
↕ 13cm (5in)	
↕ 13cm (5in)	
↕ 13cm (5in)	26cm (10in)
↕ 13cm (5in)	
↕ 13cm (5in)	26cm (10in)
↕ 13cm (5in)	13cm (5in)

CALCULATING THE NUMBER OF SECTIONS IN THE BLIND:

❀ Each fold is made up of 2 sections.

❀ We need to divide 117cm (45in) by the number of sections we need. For any blind this will always be an odd number. In our blind, each section will be 13cm (5in) and we have 9 sections.

❀ The solid lines represent the Roman blind tape placement lines.

❀ The dotted lines represent the fold lines.

❀ Each section measures 13cm (5in), so this is multiplied by 2, giving 26cm (10in) between the Roman blind tape placement lines.

❀ The bottom section is 13cm (5in) deep.

❀ Check your calculations by adding 26 + 26 + 26 + 26 + 13 = 117cm (10 + 10 + 10 + 10 + 5 = 45in).

❀ To this finished length add 6cm (2¼in) for top and bottom hems.

1 ATTACH LINING TO MAIN FABRIC

Sew the main fabric and lining fabric together, right sides facing, along the two side edges, with a 1.5cm (⅝in) seam allowance. As the main fabric is wider, you'll have to pull the lining across to make the raw edges line up for the second seam. You will have made a big tube. Turn it inside out and press seams to the inside. Centre the lining so that the two margins of main fabric are even; they should measure about 2.2cm (⅞in).

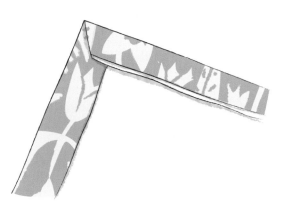

2 TURN DOWN TOP HEM

At the top of the blind press 1cm (⅜in) towards the wrong side of the blind. Tuck the corners in so that the raw edges don't stick out.

3 ATTACH LOOP TAPE

Separate the two sides of the hook and loop tape. Pin and machine-stitch the loop side along the top edge of the blind, sewing close to the edge of the tape. Stitch again along the lower edge of the loop tape. This will cover up the raw edge that you pressed down in Step 2.

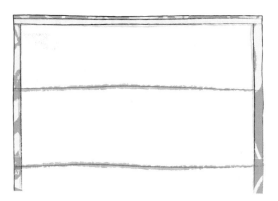

4 MARK POSITIONS OF BLIND TAPE

The function of the Roman blind tape is to hold the dowels, which create the folds in the blind when it is pulled up.

Mark the intervals where the blind tape will be sewn with a pin at either edge. Iron the blind at these points so that you then have a crease along the width of the blind. This will act as a stitching guide for sewing on the blind tape.

5 FINISH ONE END OF TAPE

Cut a length of blind tape that is 10cm (4in) longer than the width of your blind. Fold one end over twice to the wrong side to hide the raw edges and hand-sew in place as shown.

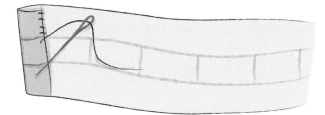

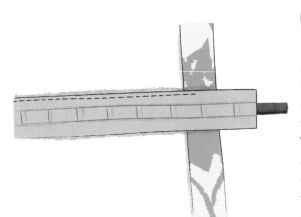

6 ATTACH BLIND TAPE

First, making sure that the lining and main fabric are lying flat, pin the blind tape, starting with the closed end, along the width of the blind over one of the creases. Align the top edge of the tape with the crease (make sure that loops face upwards). Topstitch the tape to the blind, through all layers, along the upper edge of the tape only. (The open end of the blind tape will extend past the edge of the blind; this will be trimmed later.)

Repeat this step for the other folds in your blind.

MAKE CHANNEL FOR BATTEN

The function of the flat batten is to add weight to the bottom of the blind.

Along the bottom edge of the blind, fold then press 5cm (2in) towards the wrong side of the blind, then turn under a 1cm (⅜in) hem to hide the raw edges. Pin, then topstitch close to the edge of the top fold through all layers. This will create a channel for the batten to slot into.

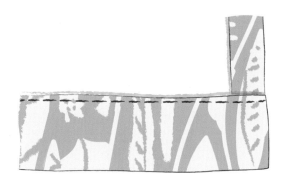

8 INSERT BATTEN AND DOWELS

Slide each dowel into the blind tape. Trim the excess tape, fold it over twice to hide the raw edge, then hand-stitch in place, keeping it free of the blind.

Slide the flat batten into the bottom channel and secure each end of the channel with small, neat ladder stitches (see page 23).

9 ATTACH TOP BATTEN

Before you secure the top batten to the window frame, stick the hook part of the hook and loop tape to one side of it. The stickiness can reduce over time, so use small tacks or a staple gun to reinforce it.

Fix the batten to the window frame with screws and rawl plugs, using an electric drill, fixing them through the front of the batten, through the hook and loop tape. Or, if you wish the blind to hang from inside the window frame, insert the screws vertically. (If you are not skilled at DIY, it is best to hire a handyman to fix the batten for you.)

Insert the screw eyes into the bottom of the batten, so that they point downwards. They should be about 25–30cm (10–12in) apart, but this distance will depend on the size of your window; there should always be one at either end.

The number of cords you need will equal the number of screw eyes.

Lauren's Tip

PAINT THE WOODEN BATTEN THE SAME COLOUR AS YOUR WINDOW FRAME BEFORE FIXING IT INTO POSITION TO MAKE IT BLEND IN A BIT MORE.

10 INSERT BLIND CORDS

Mark the positions of your blind cords on the lowest strip of blind tape; they should correspond to the positions of the screw eyes. Cut each length of cord twice the length of the blind plus the distance it will have to cross to reach the side of the window (you will have some left over, but this is better than running short). Tie a blind cord to the loop at each position, knotting the end securely (see below), then thread it through the loops on each of the remaining tapes.

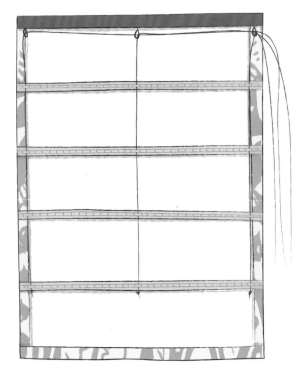

Lauren's Tip

TO MAKE SURE THE KNOTS IN YOUR CORDS DON'T COME LOOSE, FASTEN THEM WITH A FEW HAND STITCHES USING WHITE THREAD.

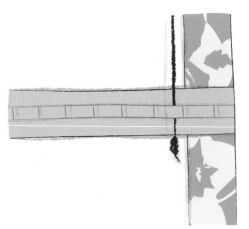

11 HANG UP THE BLIND

Get someone to help you hang the blind: one of you to support the blind, the other to hang it. Stick the loop tape to the hook tape on the batten, then thread each cord through the screw eyes towards one side (either right or left) of the window, as shown in the drawing. (You will need to stand behind the blind to do this.)

When all the cords have been threaded through the screw eyes, cut them off about halfway down the blind. This is where the blind pull will hang when the blind is closed, so don't position it too high; otherwise you will have to reach to pull the blind open.

Make sure the cords are the same length at the side, then push them through the blind pull and secure them with a knot.

Screw the cleat to the side of the window frame so that the cords can be secured when the blind is raised.

Variation BLIND WITH TRIMMED EDGE

Once you have constructed the blind, you may wish to hand-sew a trim to the lower edge. Tear-drop beads look really elegant; or for a more informal, fun look, try a pompom trim.

Position the trim just behind the front edge so that most of it is visible from the front, and sew it in place using ladder stitch (see page 23) or backstitch (see page 23) to make it really secure.

ADVENTURE SHORTS
For a Boy

These fun adventure shorts are great for boys who love to play and explore. The ample pockets (you can choose side pouch-style pockets or front square pockets, as shown on page 170) are perfect for keeping little toys safe or holding other bits and bobs that boys love to collect. The side pockets and hem facing also offer a chance to add contrast to the shorts with a bold or patterned fabric, making the shorts really individual to your child. The partly elasticated waistband makes them comfortable and easy to pull up and down, while the mock fly front adds a stylish touch.

For Practising
INSERTING ELASTIC

ATTACHING PATCH POCKETS

SEE ALSO:
TOPSTITCHING, P.219

Size
see page 208

Materials

FOR MAIN VERSION

Up to 110cm (43in) of main fabric, 114cm (45in) wide, or 90cm (36in) of main fabric 152cm (60in) wide

40cm (16in) of contrast fabric

2.5cm- (1in-) wide elastic; you will need half the measurement of the child's waist.

Coordinating thread

10cm (4in) of iron-on interfacing at least 22cm (9in) wide

FOR VARIATION

20cm (8in) of contrast fabric

Other materials as for main version

1 CUT OUT AND PREPARE FABRIC

Following the pattern, cut out the pattern pieces in your chosen fabrics using the cutting layout on page 211. Transfer all pattern markings. Iron the interfacing onto the wrong side of the front waistband section.

2 PARTIALLY SEW SIDE SEAMS

With right sides facing, sew the front and back sections together at the side edges, using a 1.5cm (⅝in) seam allowance (used throughout this project) stopping 3cm (1¼in) from the top. (This is where the front waistband will be joined later.) Press the seams open and finish off the edges.

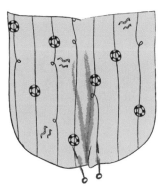

3 FORM POCKET PLEATS

On each of the four pocket pieces, pin two pleats along the bottom edge by bringing each of the side notches towards the centre notch; tack these in place.

4 JOIN POCKET FRONT AND BACK

Pin two pocket pieces together with right sides facing; hand-tack if you wish. Taking the normal seam allowance, stitch them together, leaving a 4cm (1½in) gap along the top edge. Trim the top corners diagonally and notch the curved edges to reduce bulk. Repeat with the other two pocket pieces.

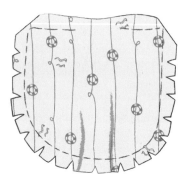

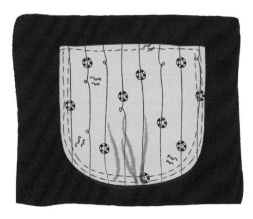

5 ATTACH POCKET TO SHORTS

Turn each pocket right side out and press it flat along the seams (avoiding the unpressed pleats), turning in the raw edges along the gap opening to hide them. Topstitch along the upper edge of the pocket, 3mm (⅛in) from the edge; this will also secure the opening edges.

Place the pocket on the right side of one of the shorts panels, matching the top corners of the pocket with the two dot markings. Pin it in place (hand-tack if you wish) and then topstitch it in place with two lines of stitching, 3mm (⅛in) and 1cm (⅜in) from the edge of the pocket.

6 MAKE POCKET FLAPS

Sew two of the pocket flap pieces together with right sides facing, along their curved edges. Notch the curves.

Turn the flap right side out and press it flat. Topstitch two lines as for the pocket. These are purely decorative but give a really neat finish.

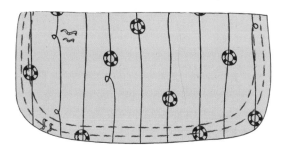

7 ATTACH POCKET FLAP

Position the flap on the shorts 1cm (³/₈in) above the pocket with the flap turned upwards. Pin then zigzag-stitch it in place.

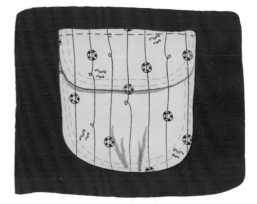

8 TOPSTITCH THE FLAP

Now fold the flap over so that it sits over the pocket; topstitch it in place 3mm (¹/₈in) from the folded edge.

Repeat Steps 6–8 with the remaining flap pieces.

9 JOIN INNER LEG SEAMS

With right sides facing, pin the inner leg seams, then stitch. Press the seams open and finish off the seam allowances.

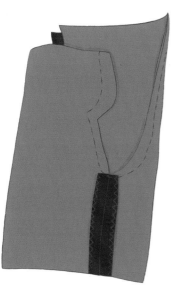

10 JOIN CROTCH SEAM

Turn one leg wrong side out and slip the other one, right side out, inside it, so that their right sides are facing. Pin the crotch seam together, matching the inner leg seams and notches; hand-tack if you wish. Stitch, pivoting at the dot marking at the bottom of the curve that will form the mock fly front. Press the seam allowances and fly extension tab to the left. Finish off the seam allowances together. Trim the inner leg seam allowances where they meet the crotch seam to reduce bulk.

11 STITCH MOCK FLY FRONT

Turn the shorts right side out. At the front of the shorts pin the centre point notches together. Fold, then press the fly tab to the wearer's left side, then pin it in place.

Draw a stitch guideline with a chalk marker on the front section. Using your fingertips, locate the edge of the fly tab underneath, then trace a line about 1cm (3/8in) inside this, starting at the point where the crotch seam curves upwards.

Stitch on top of your chalk marking to hold the fly tab in place, reverse stitch at the beginning and end to secure.

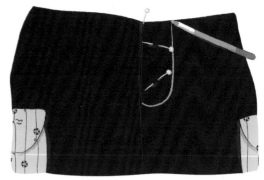

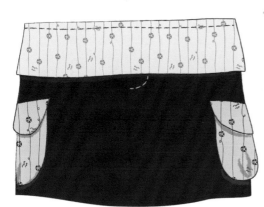

12 ATTACH FRONT WAISTBAND

With right sides facing, line up the waistband section with the top edge of the front of the shorts, matching up the centre notches. Stitch the seam, then press the seam allowances up towards the waistband.

With right sides facing, sew the rest of the side seams. Press them open. This step will join the back and front waistband sections.

13 MAKE CASING IN BACK WAISTBAND

Turn the shorts wrong side out. Fold then press 1.5cm (5/8in) to the wrong side along the top edge of the entire waistband, then fold and press again by another 3cm (1 1/4in). This will hide the raw edges along the top of the shorts.

On the back waistband, topstitch the fold in place 3mm (1/8in) from the top edge and the same distance from the lower edge. Both lines of topstitching need to stop at the side seams.

14 INSERT ELASTIC, COMPLETE WAISTBAND

Attach a safety pin to one end of the elastic and feed it through the casing. Pin then machine-stitch the elastic at the side seams, stitching through all layers.

Topstitch the front waistband in place with two lines of stitching to match the waistband on the back.

Lauren's Tip

PRESSING THE HEM SECTIONS WILL BE EASIER IF YOU DO THIS ON A SLEEVE BOARD.

15 JOIN HEM SECTIONS

Join the front and back hem sections at their side edges, with right sides facing. Along the top (un-notched) edge of each hem section press 1.5cm (⅝in) to the wrong side.

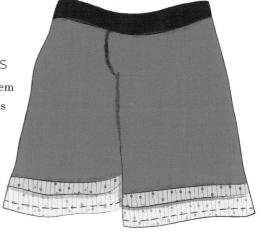

16 ATTACH HEM SECTIONS TO SHORTS

Turn the shorts wrong side out. With the right side of the hem facing the wrong side of the shorts, match up the side seams and notches. Pin in place then sew.

Press each hem section away from the shorts.

17 FINISH HEM SECTIONS

Turn the shorts right side out, then press the hem section up towards the shorts. Topstitch it in place with two lines of stitching 3mm (⅛in) away from each edge.

✳ *Variation* SHORTS WITH FRONT SQUARE POCKETS

PREPARE POCKETS ▷

Before joining the front and back sections, as described in
Step 2 of the main version, join two of the pocket pieces.
Pin them together with right sides facing, and stitch, along
the curved, front and bottom edges as shown. Notch the
curved edge and trim diagonally across the bottom corner.
Repeat with the other two pocket pieces.

Turn each pocket right side out and press it flat. Topstitch
twice along the curved edge, placing one line of stitching
about 3mm (⅛in) from the edge and the other 1cm (⅜in)
away from it.

◁ ATTACH POCKETS TO SHORT FRONTS

Place one shorts front piece right side up and position one pocket
on top as shown. Pin them together, matching the notches; tack
if you wish. Topstitch the pocket along its front and bottom edges
with two lines of stitching, placing one line 3mm (⅛in) from the
edge and the other 1cm (⅜in) away from it.

Repeat to attach the other pocket to the remaining shorts front
piece.

Complete the shorts following Steps 2 and 10–17.

PYJAMA BOTTOMS
For Cosy Comfort

A basic in everyone's wardrobe, a pair of lovely, comfy PJ bottoms in a soft cotton fabric are easy to wear and easy to make, too. This project is a really good place to get to grips with following a garment pattern, as you don't need to worry too much about getting the fit right. The simple shorts version has a contrast panel at the hem; the full-length version (see page 176) has handy contrast pockets in the side seams.

Size
see page 208

Materials

FOR SHORT VERSION

1.2m (1⅜yd) of main fabric at least 114cm (45in) wide, such as medium-weight cotton

60cm (¾yd) of contrast fabric at least 114cm (45in) wide, such as medium-weight cotton

Coordinating thread

Piece of 2cm (¾in) elastic half your waist measurement

Piece of iron-on interfacing at least 5cm (2in) square

FOR FULL-LENGTH VERSION

2.4m (2⅝yd) of main fabric at least 114cm (45in) wide, as for short version

60cm (¾yd) of contrast fabric at least 114cm (45in) wide, as for short version

Coordinating thread

Piece of 2cm (¾in) elastic half your waist measurement

Piece of iron-on interfacing at least 5cm (2in) square

1 CUT OUT FABRIC PIECES

Following the cutting layout on page 212 and using the pattern, cut out the fabric pieces (see page 26) in the two fabrics. Also from the contrast fabric cut two strips 50 x 5cm (20 x 2in) for ties. Transfer all pattern markings onto the fabric.

2 SEW INSIDE LEG SEAMS

Pin a front piece and a back piece together, right sides facing, along the inside leg edges. Stitch the seam with a 1.5cm (⅝in) seam allowance (used throughout). Press the seam allowances open and finish them off. Repeat to join the other inside leg seam.

For Practising

INSERTING ELASTIC
INSERTING POCKETS

SEE ALSO
MAKING A BUTTONHOLE, P.41
HEMMING, P.44

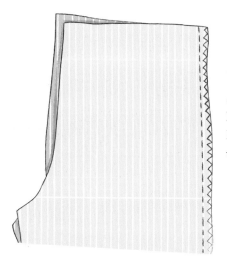

3 SEW SIDE SEAMS

Pin and stitch the side seams, with right sides facing. Finish off the seam allowances together and press them towards the front.

4 ADD CONTRAST BORDER

Pin and stitch the front and back panels together at the side edges; press the seams open. At the top (un-notched) edge of the panels press 1.5cm (⅝in) to the wrong side (see tip on page 175).

Turn the pyjamas wrong side out and pin the border, also wrong side out, around the lower edge of each leg, matching side seams and notches and with the pressed-back edge at the top, as shown. Tack if you wish, then stitch 1.5cm (⅝in) from the lower edge.

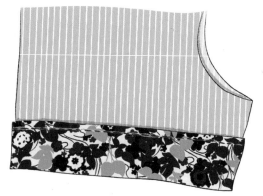

5 FINISH ATTACHING BORDER

Press the border down, away from the pyjamas. Turn the pyjamas right side out, and fold the border up over each leg; press it so that the seam you stitched in Step 4 is at the edge. Pin and tack, then topstitch the border in place 2mm (scant ⅛in) from its top (pressed-under) edge.

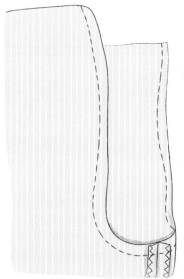

6 SEW CROTCH SEAM

Turn one leg right side out. Place it inside the other leg (turned wrong side out) so that the right sides of the fabric are facing. Match up inner leg seams and front and back notches and pin in place; tack if you wish, then stitch the seam. Press the seam to one side and finish off the raw edges together.

Lauren's Tip

TO MAKE IT EASIER TO PRESS THE SEAM ALLOWANCE TO THE WRONG SIDE, MACHINE-TACK 1.5CM (⅝IN) FROM THE RAW EDGE AND USE THIS AS A PRESSING GUIDE. THEN REMOVE THE TACKING STITCHES.

7 MAKE THE BUTTONHOLES

Turn under and press 3cm (1¼in) along the upper edge of the pyjama bottoms, then turn under and press another 3cm (1¼in). This will be stitched later to form the casing for the elastic.

Now open out the folds. Iron the small piece of interfacing to the marking for the buttonhole on each side of the crotch seam. Stitch two buttonholes (see page 41) and cut them open.

8 STITCH THE CASING

Re-fold the casing and pin it in place. Topstitch 2.7cm (generous 1in) down from the top folded edge, leaving a gap of 8cm (3in) along the back. Repeat with a line of topstitching 3mm (⅛in) from the top; this will stop the elastic from twisting.

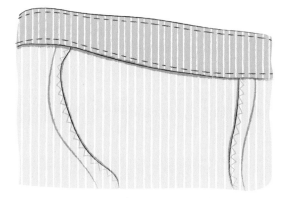

⑨ ATTACH WAIST TIES TO ELASTIC

Press each tie piece in half lengthways, wrong sides together.
Open out this fold and fold the raw edges in to meet the crease.
Re-fold the tie, enclosing the raw edges. Topstitch close to the
turned-in edges. Tie a little knot at one end of each tie.

Attach the unknotted ends of the ties to the elastic with two or three
rows of zigzag stitch.

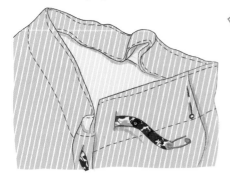

⑩ FEED ELASTIC AND TIES THROUGH CASING

Attach a safety pin to each end of the waist ties. Feed the ties
through the gap in the casing you left at the back and out through the
buttonholes at the front. Pin the elastic to the top edge of the pyjamas
at each side seam, then topstitch it in place. Topstitch the gap in the
casing to close it. (You will have to stretch the elastic to make the
fabric lie flat when you do this.)

✳ *Variation* FULL-LENGTH PYJAMA BOTTOMS WITH POCKETS

ATTACH POCKETS TO LEGS ▷

Cut out four pocket pieces from the contrast fabric. Finish
off the raw edges of these pieces individually; repeat on the
side seam edges of the front and back leg pieces. Pin one
pocket piece to each of the leg pieces with right sides facing
and with the marked dots matching. Sew each pocket piece
in place and press the pockets outwards.

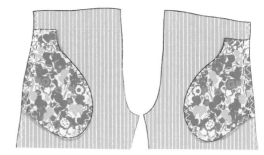

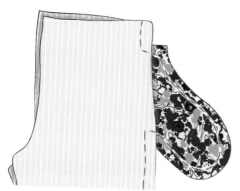

◁ JOIN SIDE SEAMS

Join the side seams as in Step 3 of the main version, sewing
around the pocket edges as part of this seam, pivoting at the dots.

HEM THE PYJAMAS

Turn up and press 2.5cm (1in) on the bottom edge of each leg,
then turn up and press another 2.5cm (1in). Topstitch the hems
in place 2.3cm (⅞in) from the bottom edge.

Improvers
More Tricky

✳ ✳ ✳ ✳

YOKE TOP
With Back Neck Opening

I love this little top, as the yoke offers lots of opportunity to add detail and contrast. In the version shown here, the main part of the bodice is gathered at centre front and the yoke itself accentuated with piping. In the variation on page 186 the fullness is taken in with a few crisp pleats instead. Either way, the semi-fitted, A-line style is relatively easy to work with in terms of getting the fit right. The comfortable, slightly wide neckline has a small stand collar. Make the top in a crisp cotton print, as here, or in lightweight silk, as shown in the variation, for a dressier look.

Size
see page 208

Materials

FOR MAIN VERSION

1.5m (1⅝yd) of lightweight printed cotton, 152cm (60in) wide, or 1.9m (2yd) of 114cm (45in) wide cotton

4 x 15mm (⅝in) buttons

1m (1⅛yd) of 18–20mm (¾in) bias binding

70cm (⅞yd) purchased contrasting piping (optional)

16cm (6¼in) of lightweight iron-on interfacing at least 33cm (13in) wide

Coordinating thread

FOR VARIATION

1m (1⅛yd) lightweight fabric (width) for main bodice section. Should have good draping quality; suggested fabrics: silk crêpe de Chine, lightweight viscose

70cm (¾yd) contrasting lightweight fabric (width) for yoke section

16cm (6¼in) of lightweight iron-on interfacing at least 33cm (13in) wide

Coordinating thread

1 CUT OUT FABRIC PIECES

Using the pattern and following the cutting layout (see page 213), cut out all sections of your top. Transfer all pattern markings onto your fabric.

Cut one collar piece from interfacing and two strips of interfacing, each 17 x 4cm (6¾ x 1½in). Iron the collar piece to one collar section (this will be the outer collar) and iron the strips to the centre back of the inner yoke pieces.

For Practising

ATTACHING A YOKE
ATTACHING A STAND COLLAR
STAY STITCHING
UNDERSTITCHING
SEE ALSO:
PLEATS AND GATHERS, P.60
FRENCH SEAMS, P.35
BUTTONHOLES, P.41
LADDER STITCH, P.23
HEMMING, P.44

2 PREPARE FRONT BODICE

Using a long stitch length, sew two rows of gathering stitches between the two dots at the top of the front bodice 5mm (¼in) and 1.2cm (½in) from the edge, leaving long thread tails. Set this section aside.

3 JOIN SIDE SEAMS

Matching notches, pin and stitch the side seams. Finish off the raw edges (see page 34).

4 ATTACH BIAS BINDING TO ARMHOLES

Apply bias binding (see page 54) to the armhole edges of the main bodice, folding it over twice so that the binding is on the inside. (The yoke armholes do not need binding as they will be finished with the lining.)

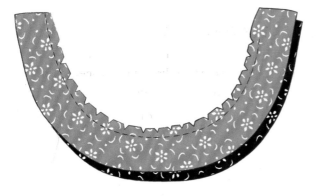

Lauren's Tip

TO MAKE THE INSIDES OF THE TOP REALLY NEAT, TRY A FRENCH SEAM AS DESCRIBED (SEE PAGE 35) AT THE SIDE SEAMS.

5 JOIN INNER AND OUTER COLLAR SECTIONS

Place the inner and outer (interfaced) collar sections together with right sides facing. Pin (tack if you like) and sew them together along the shorter edges. Trim the seam allowance in half and notch it as shown to reduce bulk.

6 UNDERSTITCH INNER COLLAR

Press the seam allowances towards the inner (non-interfaced) collar. Now, working on the right side, stitch through the inner collar and seam allowances, close to the seamline. Press the collar along the seamline so that the inner collar rolls to the inside; the understitching, as it is called, helps you to do this and keeps the seam allowances in place.

7 NEATEN INNER COLLAR EDGE

You now need to press under 1.5cm (⅝in) along the bottom edge of the inner collar, which is a little tricky as this is a curved edge. You can make this easier by stitching along the bottom edge at this distance and using the stitching as a pressing guide.

8 JOIN FRONT AND BACK YOKE

Pin and stitch the outer front and back yoke sections together at the shoulders, with right sides facing and a 1.5cm (⅝in) seam allowance (used throughout). Repeat for the inner yoke sections. Press all seams open.

At the bottom edge of the front inner yoke (only), machine-tack 1.5cm (⅝in) from the raw edge; using this as a pressing guide, press the fabric to the wrong side.

9 ATTACH OUTER COLLAR TO OUTER YOKE

With right sides facing, pin (tack if you wish) the outer collar to the outer yoke, matching the notches on the collar to the shoulder seams and to the notches on the yoke neckline. Stitch the seam.

Trim the seam allowances in half and then notch them to reduce bulk. Press them towards the collar.

Lauren's Tip

AS THIS IS A CURVED SEAM YOU MAY NEED TO FIDDLE AROUND TO GET THE RAW EDGES TO LINE UP. INSERT THE PINS PERPENDICULAR TO THE EDGE AND USE PLENTY OF THEM. AS YOU STITCH, MAKE SURE THAT THE FABRIC UNDERNEATH IS LYING FLAT AND THAT THE RAW EDGES REMAIN ALIGNED. OR, IF YOU PREFER, TACK THE SEAM BEFORE STITCHING.

10 JOIN INNER AND OUTER YOKE AT ARMHOLES

Pin (tack if you wish) and sew the outer and inner yoke sections together at each armhole with right sides facing, stopping when you reach the pressed-under seam allowance at the bottom edge of the front inner yoke. Trim the seam allowances and notch them to reduce bulk.

11 UNDERSTITCH ARMHOLE SEAM

Turn the yoke right side out. Understitch the seam allowances to the inner yoke as for the collar in Step 6. Press the seam flat, ensuring that the understitching is on the inside of the garment.

12 JOIN OUTER AND INNER YOKE AND COLLAR AT BACK OPENING

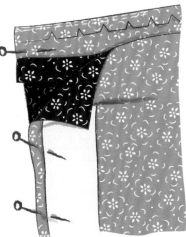

You are now going to sew the edges of the back opening where the buttonholes will go. First fold the inner collar wrong side out and pin it together so that the right sides of both collars are facing. Pin the raw edges together.

Line up the inner and outer back yoke pieces, right sides facing. The top edge of the inner yoke should overlap the seam allowances at the collar. Pin (tack if you wish) and stitch all the way from the top edge of the collar to the bottom of the back yoke on both right and left opening edges. Turn the yoke right side out.

13 SEW INNER COLLAR TO INNER YOKE

Pin the inner collar to the inner yoke, ensuring that the raw edge of the yoke is concealed. Tack if you wish. Using ladder stitch as shown (see page 23), sew the inner collar to the inner yoke.

14 MAKE THE BUTTONHOLES

Following the pattern markings, make four buttonholes (see page 41) in the yoke on the wearer's left-hand side.

15 ADD OPTIONAL PIPING

Cut two lengths of piping, each about 4cm (1½in) longer than the lower edge of the front and back yoke. Pin one to the right side of the back bodice section along its top edge with raw edges matching. Machine-tack it in place, leaving the ends unstitched where they meet the stitching joining the binding at the armhole edge.

Apply the piping in the same way to the bottom edge of the outer yoke section.

16 JOIN OUTER YOKE AND BODICE

With right sides facing, pin (tack if you wish) and stitch the front outer yoke section to the bodice front, matching centre points, distributing the gathers evenly, and taking in the piping, if used, at the same time. At each side of the top edge of the bodice, the bottom edge of the yoke will have a 1.5cm (⅝in) overhang. This is normal and will ensure that the binding around the armhole is hidden.

Press the seam allowances towards the yoke.

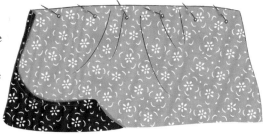

17 SEW INNER YOKE TO FRONT BODICE

Fold under the seam allowance on the inner yoke that you pressed under in Step 9. Pin it over the seam joining the bodice and outer yoke, enclosing those seam allowances, and sew it in place with ladder stitch. Turn the ends of the piping in at the armhole edges to conceal them, trimming them if necessary.

YOKE TOP

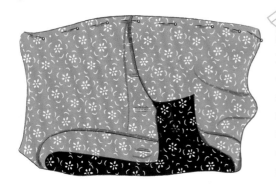

18 JOIN YOKE TO BACK BODICE

Place the outer and inner back yoke sections together, wrong sides facing. Placing them on a flat surface, tack them together about 3cm (1in) in from the lower edges so they lie smoothly against each other. Pin and tack them to the back bodice, right sides facing, and with the buttonhole opening side under the other side as shown. Stitch the seam, enclosing the piping, if used; turn up the piping ends (trimmed if necessary) to hide them in the seam. Finish off the seam allowances together and press them down towards the back bodice.

19 HEM GARMENT AND SEW ON BUTTONS

Turn under and press 2.5cm (1in), then another 2.5cm (1in) along the bottom edge. Topstitch the hem in place 2.3cm (⅞in) from the bottom.

Stitch the buttons on following the pattern markings.

✳ *Variation* TOP WITH PLEATED BODICE

Mark the pleats on the right side of the bodice, following the pattern markings.

FOLD THE PLEATS ▷

Starting with the centre pleat, fold the bodice as indicated by the pattern markings and pin the pleats in place. Machine-tack across the top, 1.2cm (½in) from the top edge.

MAKE BIAS BINDING FOR ARMHOLES

From the main fabric, cut 50cm (20in) of bias binding (see page 50), 18–20mm (¾in) wide. Use this to bind the armholes of the bodice section as instructed in Step 4 of the main version.

Complete the top as for the main version, Steps 3–19.

💡 *Other Variation Ideas*

✳ Use a bold contrasting patterned fabric for the main bodice with a plain fabric for the yoke sections, or vice versa.

✳ Use lace for the outer yoke, with a plain lightweight fabric underneath, to make it more of a feature.

Pick Your Pockets
SKIRT

For Practising

TUCKS, P.58
INSERTING PIPING OR OTHER TRIM, P.56
INSERTING A ZIP, P.36
LADDER STITCH, P.23
HEMMING, P.44

For me, pockets are a must to keep a few essentials to hand. With this skirt you can hide the pockets in the side seams or make them more of a feature with a front slash option, as shown on page 192. The yoke section is strengthened with interfacing and acts as a waistband. Its join with the main skirt offers a chance to add some detail, too — try adding a lace trim or some piping — while front and back tucks on the inside give the main skirt section a little fullness.

Size

see page 208

Materials

FOR MAIN VERSION

1.5m (1⅝yd) of main fabric, 114cm (45in) wide, or 1.3m (1½yd) of fabric 152cm (60in) wide

40cm (½yd) of contrast fabric for the pockets and facings

1m (1⅛yd) of piping or braid

Coordinating thread

50cm (⅝yd) of lightweight iron-on interfacing, 90cm (36in) wide

18cm (7in) zip

FOR VARIATION

1.5m (1⅝yd) of fabric as above, 114cm (45in) wide, or 1.3m (1½yd) of fabric 152cm (60in) wide

1m (1⅛yd) of piping or braid

50cm (⅝yd) of lightweight iron-on interfacing, 90cm (36in) wide

Coordinating thread

18cm (7in) zip

1 CUT OUT FABRIC PIECES

Using the pattern, cut out the pieces from the main and contrast fabrics and interfacing using the cutting layout on page 214. Transfer all markings and notches. Iron the interfacing onto the wrong side of the front and back inner yoke sections.

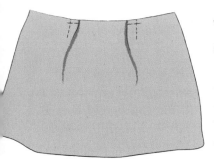

2 FORM THE TUCKS

Following the marked lines and working on the right side of the front skirt piece, fold the tucks and pin them in place. Turn the piece wrong side up and stitch the tucks for the marked length. Press both tucks towards the centre, then tack 1.2cm (½in) from the top edge.

Tuck the two back skirt sections in the same way, pressing and tacking them so that on the wrong side they point towards the centre back edge.

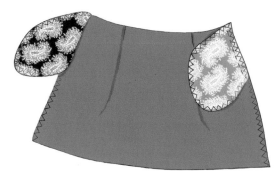

3 ATTACH POCKET PIECES

First finish off the raw edges of all four pocket pieces and the side edges of the main skirt front and back. (It won't be possible to do this once they are attached.)

With right sides facing, pin and stitch the pockets to the side edges of the main skirt sections, matching the dot markings: two to the front as shown and one to each back section. Press the pocket pieces and seam allowances away from the skirt sections. Remember to use a 1.5cm (⅝in) seam allowance (used throughout).

4 JOIN SIDE SEAMS

Place the skirt front and one skirt back together with right sides facing and side edges matching and with the pocket pieces extended. Pin them together (tack if you wish) and stitch the side seams, including the pocket edges. Start at the top edge of the skirt, pivot at the first dot marking, sewing around the pocket to the second dot marking, pivot again and continue down to the bottom edge.

Repeat to join the other back skirt section. Press all seam allowances and pockets towards the front of the skirt.

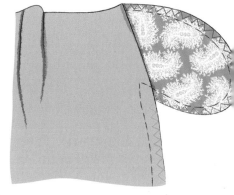

5 SEW CENTRE BACK SEAM

With right sides facing, pin and stitch the centre back seam up to the mark for the end of the zip. Press the seam open and finish off the seam allowances (see page 34).

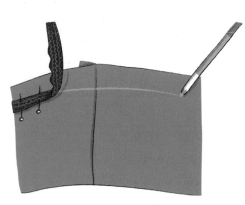

6 ASSEMBLE AND TRIM OUTER YOKE

Pin and stitch the three outer yoke sections together, right sides facing, at their side edges. Finish off the seam allowances and press the seams open.

Using a seam gauge and chalk pencil, mark the 1.5cm (⅝in) seam allowance along the right side of the lower edge of the yoke. Position the trim, right side down, along this line as shown, so that only its edge will be caught in the seam later. Pin and tack it in place. (If you prefer to use piping, see the instructions on page 56.) Finish off the centre back raw edges of the yoke.

7 ATTACH OUTER YOKE TO MAIN SKIRT AND INSERT ZIP

Pin (tack if you wish) and stitch the outer yoke to the main skirt sections, with right sides facing and side seams and centre front matching. This may be tricky as the yoke is curved, so take extra care to ensure that the raw edges line up.

Following the standard zip insertion instructions on page 36, insert the zip in the centre back seam.

8 ATTACH INNER YOKE

Pin and stitch the three inner yoke sections together, with right sides facing, at their side edges. Finish off the seam allowances and press the seams open.

Machine-tack 1.5cm (⅝in) from the bottom edge. Use this stitching line as a guide, press the seam allowance towards the wrong side.

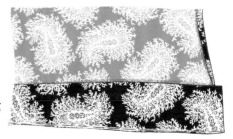

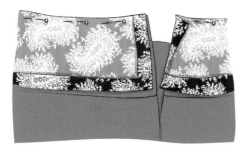

9 JOIN INNER AND OUTER YOKE

Pin the top edges of the inner and outer yoke together with right sides facing, matching the side seams and centre points; tack if you wish.

Turn back the seam allowance on the centre back edges of the inner yoke as shown. Stitch the seam, catching in these folded edges as you do so.

10 SEW INNER YOKE IN PLACE

Press the seam allowances towards the inner yoke. Turn the yoke right side up. Understitch the inner yoke and seam allowances 2mm (scant ⅛in) from the seamline. This keeps the inner yoke inside the skirt.

Turn the inner yoke to the inside of the skirt and press it in place. Hand-sew it to the outer yoke and to the zip tape around the pressed-under edges, using ladder stitch (see page 23).

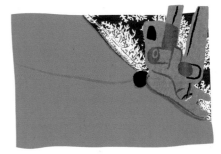

11 HEM THE SKIRT

Turn under and press 1.2cm (½in) along the lower edge of the skirt, then turn under and press another 1.2cm (½in). Topstitch in place 1cm (⅜in) from the bottom.

✺ *Variation* SKIRT WITH SLASH FRONT POCKETS

Cut the appropriate fabric pieces and transfer the pattern markings. Apply interfacing to the inner yoke pieces. Form the tucks as for the main version, Step 2.

ATTACH POCKET FRONTS TO SKIRT ▷

Pin (tack if you wish) and stitch the front pocket sections to the skirt front along their top edges with right sides facing. Notch the seam allowances to enable them to lie flat, then finish them off together. Press each pocket front away from the main skirt section and then fold it over and press it flat, so that it sits behind the skirt.

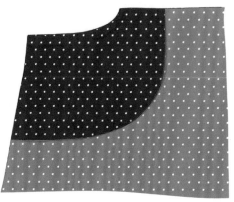

◁ ATTACH POCKET BACKS

Pin the pocket backs to the pocket fronts along their lower edges with right sides facing. Tack if you wish, then stitch them together, ensuring the main skirt front section is folded out of the way. Press the seam flat. Finish off the seam allowances together.

Place the skirt front wrong side up. Adjust one pocket so that it lies flat against the skirt and pin and tack it in place along the side and top edges. Repeat with the other pocket.

JOIN SIDE SEAMS

With right sides facing, pin (tack if you wish) and stitch the skirt back sections to the skirt front section. Press the seams open and finish off the seam allowances.

Complete the skirt following Steps 5–12 of the main version.

✼ ✼ ✼ ✼

RIBBON HANDBAG
With Changeable Strap

This project was inspired by a bag that I made as a teenager from a bunch of beautiful embroidered ribbons my mum brought back from New York for me. They all looked so good and colourful together that I wanted to make something that would let me see and use them all the time. I stitched them onto a plain fabric and turned it into a little, semicircular going-out bag.

For the bag shown here, I added a gusset for extra depth. The bag is fully lined with a zip closure and has a matching strap, which attaches to the bag with a button and buttonhole fastening. For the variation on page 199, I recycled a vintage scarf by folding it into a strap and tying it onto the bag.

For Practising

CREATING YOUR OWN FABRIC FROM RIBBONS AND TRIMS

INSERTING A LINING

SEE ALSO:

INSERTING A ZIP, P.36
BUTTONHOLES, P.41
LADDER STITCH, P.23

Finished Size

Approx. 40cm (16in) wide by 19cm (7½in) deep

Materials

FOR MAIN VERSION

30cm (⅜yd) of calico for base backing fabric

50cm (⅝yd) of lining fabric, any width, such as light- to medium-weight cotton

30cm (⅜yd) of contrast fabric, such as medium-weight, hard-wearing cotton, any width, for gusset and handle

30cm (⅜yd) medium-weight iron-on interfacing

Selection of ribbons

and trims (total of approx. 6m [6⅝yd] but can be variety of different lengths between 10 and 25cm [4 and 10in])

2 metal D-rings

36cm (14in) zip

Coordinating thread

FOR VARIATION

Materials as for main version, plus:

Vintage scarf; the one I used measured 50 x 50cm (20 x 20in) and produced a handle about 70cm (27in) long

1 CUT OUT FABRIC PIECES

Using the pattern pieces, cut out all the pieces for the bag in the appropriate fabrics. Transfer the pattern markings. Apply interfacing to the main section of the strap.

2 ATTACH THE RIBBONS

Place the ribbons and trims over the front and back base backing fabric sections, rearranging them until you get a design that you really love. (The two sides needn't be the same.) You will have a little bit of ribbon sticking out over the edges; this will be trimmed back later. Pin the ribbons in place and then topstitch them down by machine. You may prefer to hand-stitch those with curved or delicate edges.

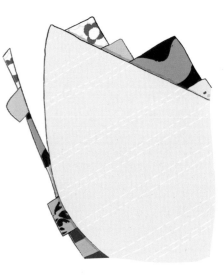

3 TRIM RIBBONS AND STAY-STITCH EDGES

Once the ribbons are secured, trim their ends even with the base pieces and stitch all the way around 1cm (³⁄₈in) from the raw edge.

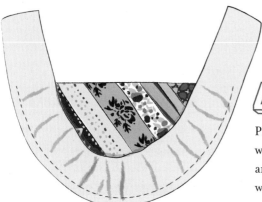

4 JOIN BOTTOM GUSSET AND BAG FRONT

Pin the bottom gusset to the lower edge of the front of the bag with right sides facing, matching the centre point of the gusset and the centre point of the bag. Tack if you wish, then stitch with a 1.2cm (¹⁄₂in) seam.

5 ATTACH BAG BACK

Repeat to attach the back of the bag to the free edge of the bottom gusset.

Repeat Steps 4 and 5 to assemble the bag front, back and bottom gusset of the lining.

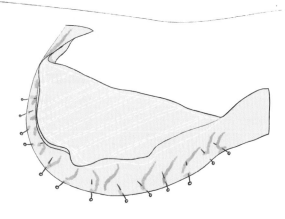

Lauren's Tip

TO ADD AN EXTRA DETAIL, INSERT A SMALL ZIP POCKET INTO THE LINING, AS FOR THE 'BIG WEEKEND BAG' (SEE PAGE 148).

6 PLACE ZIP BETWEEN GUSSET PIECES

The top gusset consists of two strips, or panels, of outer contrast fabric and two strips of lining joined by the zip.

Lay one lining panel right side up. Lay the zip on top of it, right side up, positioning it along one long edge. Place one of the outer zip panels, right side down, on top, as shown.

7 TACK HALF OF ZIP IN PLACE

Tack one half of the zip in between these two fabric strips, folding back the end of the zip to hide its top raw edge.

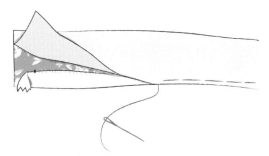

8 STITCH HALF OF ZIP INTO PANEL

With the zip foot on your machine, sew the zip in place along the long straight edge and the two short ends of these zip panels, making sure you don't accidentally catch the other half of the zip in these seams.

Turn the panels right side out.

Repeat Steps 5–7 to join the other half of the zip to the remaining zip panel and lining panel, completing the top gusset.

9 TOPSTITCH PANEL EDGES

Press the panels flat, then topstitch close to the fabric edges alongside the zip and across the ends as shown.

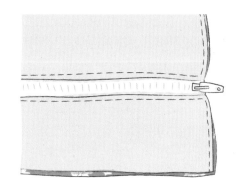

10 TACK TOP GUSSET TO MAIN BAG

Place the top gusset and main bag sections together with right sides facing. Pin and tack them together, 1.2cm (½in) from the edge.

11 JOIN MAIN PART OF LINING TO BAG

Turn both the lining and the outer bag wrong side out.

Pin and tack together along the edges of the lined top gusset, turning back the edges so right sides are facing and raw edges line up. Leave a 10cm (4in) gap along one long edge to turn right side out later. Stitch the lining and the top gusset together with a 1.2cm (½in) seam allowance. This should be done in five separate stages: the two side tabs of the bottom gusset, the long straight opening along one side of the top gusset and then the other long side (either side of the opening). Remember to reverse-stitch the beginning and end of each line. Trim the seam allowances, cut diagonally across the corners of the side tabs to reduce bulk and turn the bag right side out. Press the seams flat.

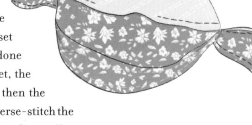

12 TOPSTITCH THE TOP GUSSET

Pin one side of the top gusset to the adjacent side of the bag. Topstitch them together 3mm (⅛in) from the seamed edge. Repeat for the other side of the top gusset. The topstitching will close up the opening you left in Step 10 and will help to keep the gusset inside the bag.

13 ATTACH THE D-RINGS

Thread the tab at each side of the bag though a D-ring and secure it by folding the tab over and sewing on a button.

14 MAKE THE STRAP

With right sides facing, sew the two straps together, taking a 1.2cm (½in) seam allowance and leaving a 5cm (2in) gap in one long side. Turn the strap right side out and press the edges. Hand-stitch the opening using ladder stitch (see page 23). Make two buttonholes in the positions marked and sew on the buttons, also following the pattern markings. Thread the strap through the D-rings and fasten the buttons to attach the strap.

✳ *Variation* VINTAGE SCARF HANDLE

▽ CREATE THE HANDLE

Fold the scarf in half to make a triangle. Starting at the folded edge, keep folding in 5cm (2in) sections until you reach the tip of the triangle. You will now have a long 5cm (2in)-wide strip. Secure the folds in place with several individual stitches along the length of the strip. Thread the ends of the strip through the D-rings on the bag and tie them in a knot.

HAVE IT YOUR WAY DRESS
For Individual Style

The beauty of making your own clothes is that there are so many ways to modify and alter the pattern to suit your own style. It may be as simple as changing the shape of a collar or more involved, such as changing the shape of a sleeve. Don't stop there, though – add pockets, alter the length, bind the hem, put piping around the collar edge . . . The possibilities are endless, so don't be scared to try!

This dress offers two collar and sleeve options. The one shown here has a rounded collar with curved sleeves and the variation on page 205 has a pointed collar with puff sleeves. It is quite fitted around the bust and waist and then flares out slightly with a gathered skirt. It looks great worn with a narrow belt; you could make a coordinating one using the instructions on pages 81–84.

Size
see page 208

Materials

FOR MAIN VERSION

2m (2¼yd) of 152cm (60in) wide fabric or 2.7m (3yd) of 114cm (45in) wide fabric

40cm (½yd) of contrast fabric, any width

50cm (⅝yd) of medium-weight iron-on interfacing, 90cm (36in) wide

56cm (22in) invisible zip

Coordinating thread

Hook and eye

FOR VARIATION

Materials as for main version, but without contrast fabric

For Practising

STAY STITCHING

ATTACHING A COLLAR

INSERTING A SLEEVE

SEE ALSO:

GATHERS, P.61

LADDER STITCH, P.23

INSERTING AN INVISIBLE ZIP, P.37

DARTS, P.48

HEMMING, P.44

1 CUT OUT AND PREPARE FABRIC PIECES

Using the pattern, cut out the appropriate fabric pieces using the cutting layout on page 215. Transfer the notches and other pattern markings, using tailor's tacks to mark the darts. Iron interfacing onto two of the four collar pieces, the front and back neck facing pieces, and the sleeve facing. A 1.5cm (⅝in) seam allowance is used throughout this project, unless otherwise stated.

STAY-STITCH THE NECKLINE

Machine-stitch along the neckline of all three bodice pieces, 1.2cm (½in) from the edge, starting at the shoulder seam and sewing towards the centre point.

3 MAKE THE DARTS

Sew the darts, following the instructions on page 48. Start with the bust darts and then make the front and back waistline darts. Press the bust darts downwards and the waist darts towards the centre.

4 MAKE THE COLLAR

Place each inner collar and outer collar together with right sides facing. Pin (tack if you wish) and stitch the outside edges of the collar sections from the shoulder edge to the centre front, taking 1cm (³⁄₈in) seam allowance. Notch the seam allowances to reduce bulk.

Turn both collars right side out and press them flat.

5 ATTACH COLLAR TO BODICE FRONT

Pin both collar sections to the bodice front with the wrong side of the collar facing the right side of the bodice. The centre edges of the collar will overlap slightly at the centre point. Tack the collars in place 1cm (³⁄₈in) from the neck edge.

6 JOIN FRONT AND BACK BODICE SECTIONS

With right sides facing, pin one back bodice to the front bodice at the shoulder. Stitch the shoulder seam, enclosing the edge of the collar. Repeat to join the other back bodice at the shoulder. Now join the side seams. Finish off the seam allowances. Press the side seams open and shoulder seams towards the back – this reduces excess bulk caused by the collar. It is a good idea to try the bodice on at this point to check the fit, but you'll need to get someone to pin the back opening closed. Places where the dress is too large can then be taken in and re-stitched. (See Notes about choosing the right size, page 208.)

7 CONSTRUCT THE SLEEVE

On each sleeve stitch two lines of gathering along the sleeve head between the two dots, 1cm and 1.5cm (3/8 and 5/8in) from the edge (see page 62); these will be used to ease the sleeve into the armhole.

On the top edge of each sleeve facing, press under 1.5cm (5/8in). Open out this fold, then join the underarm seam of the facing; press the seam allowances open and finish them off.

Join the underarm seam of each sleeve; press them and finish them off as for the facing.

Pin the sleeve facing to the sleeve, right sides together, along the bottom, curved edge. Tack if you wish and stitch with a 1cm (3/8in) seam allowance, pivoting at the dot. Notch the curved edges and press the seam flat, then turn the facing to the inside and press it flat.

Turn the sleeve wrong side out again and catch-stitch (used in Double Fold Invisible Hem on page 45) the folded edge of the facing to the wrong side of the sleeve.

8 INSERT SLEEVE INTO ARMHOLE

Insert each sleeve into the bodice armhole, with right sides facing, following the detailed instructions on page 62.

9 JOIN SIDE SEAMS OF SKIRT

With right sides facing, join the skirt front and back side seams. Finish off the raw edges, then press the seam allowances open. Alternatively you could use a French seam here (see page 35).

10 GATHER SKIRT AND ATTACH TO BODICE

Sew three rows of gathering stitches along the top edge of the skirt section, 1, 1.5 and 2cm (⅜, ⅝ and ¾in) from the raw edge, leaving long thread tails at each end.

Pull on the threads to gather up the skirt. Pin the skirt to the bodice at the centre notches and side seams and distribute the gathers evenly. Pin the bodice and skirt together at the centre back edges. Tack if you wish and stitch the seam. Finish off the seam allowances together and press them towards the bodice.

Lauren's Tip

DON'T WORRY ABOUT GETTING THE GATHERS EVEN WHEN YOU FIRST PULL UP THE THREADS; JUST GET SOME GATHERS TO WORK WITH. AFTER DIVIDING THE SKIRT INTO FOUR SECTIONS BY PINNING AT SIDE SEAMS AND CENTRE FRONT, START AT THE CENTRE AND EVEN OUT THE GATHERS ONE SECTION AT A TIME, PUSHING THEM OUT TO THE SIDE IF THERE ARE TOO MANY OR PULLING ON THE THREADS IF THERE ARE TOO FEW.

11 INSERT INVISIBLE ZIP

Following the instructions on page 37, insert the invisible zip. Pin and stitch the remaining centre back seam of the skirt. Finish off the raw edges, then press them open.

12 JOIN FACING SECTIONS

With right sides together, join the front and back facing sections at the shoulders. Press the seam allowances open. Finish off the bottom edge of the facing.

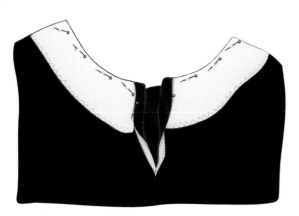

13 ATTACH FACING TO BODICE

Turn the dress right side out, with the back on top. Open the zip about 13cm (5in). Turn the inside edges of the zip towards the opening so that you can see them. Using the ordinary zip foot on your machine, sew the right side of the facing to this part of the zip, taking a 1cm (⅜in) seam allowance.

Turn the zip edge again away from the opening and pin in place. This might seem a bit strange but it will make the top of the zip really neat on the inside. Pin the rest of the facing to the neckline, matching up shoulder seams and notches. Tack if you wish and stitch the neckline seam.

14 COMPLETE NECKLINE FACING

Trim the seam allowances of the neck and clip to enable them to lie flat when you turn the facing to the inside. Understitch the seam allowances to the facing 2mm (scant ⅛in) from the seamline. Try to get as close as you can to the zip, ending the stitching about 4–5cm (2in) away from it. Press facing, ensuring it is not visible when the dress is being worn.

15 HEM THE DRESS

Turn up and press 1.2cm (½in) along the bottom edge of the dress, then turn up the same amount again. Pin or tack the hem in place, then finish it with topstitching or catch stitch.

❋ *Variation* DRESS WITH POINTED COLLAR AND PUFF SLEEVES

Cut out and assemble the dress as for the main version, Steps 1–6, applying interfacing also to the cuff pieces.

POINTED COLLAR ▷

Using the pointed collar pattern pieces, make and attach the pointed collar as for the main version, Steps 4 and 5. Before turning the collar right side out, cut diagonally across the corners to help reduce bulk. Press collar pieces flat.

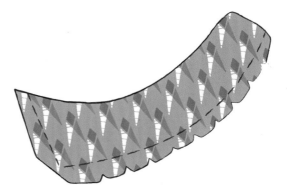

MAKE THE CUFF ▷

Press each cuff section in half lengthways, wrong sides facing. Press another 1.5cm (⅝in) to the wrong side along one edge. Open out these folds and place the ends together, right sides facing. Pin and stitch the seam; press it open.

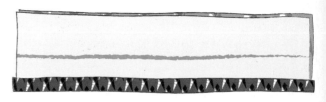

◁ CONSTRUCT THE SLEEVE

Stitch two rows of gathers between the notches on the bottom edge of the sleeve and between the two dots on the sleeve head.

Join the underarm seam of each sleeve with right sides facing. Finish off the seam allowances and press the seam open. (Alternatively, use a French seam, see page 35.)

Pull up the gathers on the lower edge of the sleeve. With right sides facing, pin the sleeve to the flat edge of the cuff, matching the notches and adjusting the gathers evenly to fit the cuff. Tack if you wish, and stitch the seam; this will be tricky, as you will have to sew around the cuff in a circle, repositioning and moving the fabric to the side as you go along.

Press the seam allowances towards the cuff. Fold the cuff to the inside of the sleeve along the centre crease, then fold under the creased seam allowance. The fold should meet the seam used to join sleeve and cuff. Hand-stitch the cuff in place using ladder stitch.

INSERT SLEEVE IN ARMHOLE

Turn the bodice wrong side out. Insert the sleeve, right side out, in the armhole. Pin it in place, matching the notches and dots, pull up the gathers and distribute them evenly. Tack the sleeve in place and stitch the seam. Finish the seam allowances together and press them towards the sleeve.

Complete the dress following Steps 9–15 of the main version.

💡 *Other Variation Ideas*

❀ Add a pocket in the side seams as for the Pick Your Pockets Skirt (page 190).

❀ Sew on patch pockets.

❀ Miss out sleeves altogether and bind armholes as shown on page 54.

Cutting layouts and Templates

The following pages and the pattern sheets (attached to the front and back of the book) can be used over and over again to make your projects in different sizes and variations. Trace your selected size from the pattern sheet using it as a master template (so that you can retain all the sizes for future use). If your measurements spread across more than one size then make the larger one as it's easier to take in the side seams if necessary. Simply lay the pattern sheet on a large table, place dressmakers' pattern paper on top, weight it down and trace off the size you need. Alternatively, using a tracing wheel and self-healing mat, lay the pattern sheet above the dressmakers' pattern paper and trace over with the tracing wheel. It's really important to also transfer all pattern markings including notches, circles, dots and grain lines (draw grain lines with a ruler to ensure that they are straight).

Once you have the pattern pieces prepared, follow the cutting layouts to place the pieces onto your fabric. Depending on the width of your fabric, there may be a more economical way to place the pieces on to avoid excessive fabric wastage, so follow the cutting layout specific to your fabric width.

ADULT SIZE GUIDE

Size	8 cm (in)	10 cm (in)	12 cm (in)	14 cm (in)	16 cm (in)	18 cm (in)
Bust	81 (32)	86 (34)	91 (36)	96 (38)	102 (40)	107 (42)
Waist	66 (26)	71 (28)	76 (30)	81 (32)	86 (34)	91 (36)
Hip	91 (36)	96 (38)	102 (40)	107 (42)	112 (44)	117 (46)

CHILDREN SIZE GUIDE

Size (Age)	2 cm (in)	3 cm (in)	4 cm (in)	5 cm (in)	6 cm (in)	7 cm (in)	8 cm (in)
Chest	53 (20¾)	55 (21½)	57 (22½)	59 (23¼)	61 (24)	63 (24¾)	67 (26¼)
Waist	52 (20½)	53 (20¾)	54 (21¼)	55 (21½)	57 (22½)	58 (22½)	60 (23½)
Hip	56 (22)	58 (22½)	60 (23½)	62 (24½)	65 (25½)	68 (26¾)	70 (27½)

SIMPLE SLEEVELESS TOP

A – front bodice
B – back bodice
C – front panel
D – back panel

1.5m (60in) wide 80cm (31½in) (60cm [23½in] for variation)
MAIN FABRIC

1.1m (45in) wide 1.5m (59in)(1.2m [47¼in] for variation)
MAIN FABRIC

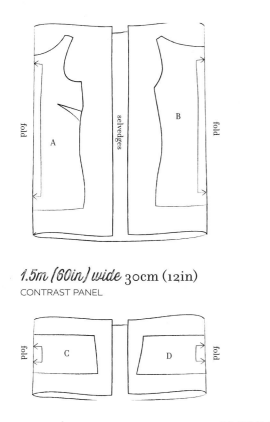

1.5m (60in) wide 30cm (12in)
CONTRAST PANEL

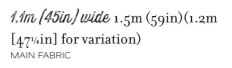

1.1m (45in) wide 40cm (15¾in)
CONTRAST PANEL

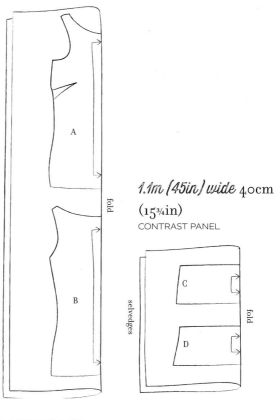

GIRL'S SUMMERTIME SET

1.1m (45in) and 1.5m (60in) wide

You'll need the length of the top x 2.
For one pocket include a contrast material
20 x 40cm (8 x 15¾in)

A – bodice front
B – bodice back
C – heart patch pocket

1.1m (45in) and 1.5m (60in) wide

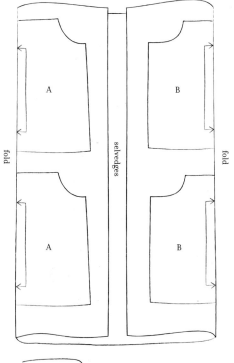

ADVENTURE SHORTS

A – shorts front
B – shorts back
C – front pocket
D – side patch pocket
E – side patch pocket flap
F – front hem facing
G – hem facing
H – front waistband

1.1m (45in) and 1.5m (60in) wide, 40cm (16in)

CONTRAST FABRIC

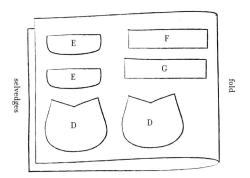

1.1m (45in) wide, 1.1m (43in)

MAIN FABRIC

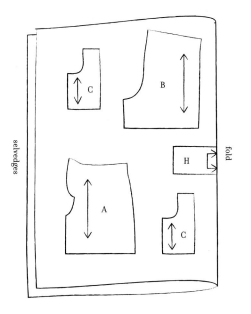

1.5m (60in) wide, 90cm (36in)

MAIN FABRIC

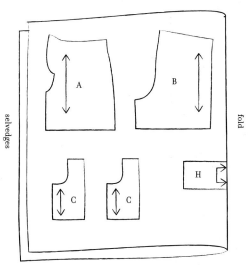

PYJAMA BOTTOMS

Short version

1.1m (45in) and 1.5m (60in) wide, 1.2m (1³⁄₈yd)

MAIN FABRIC

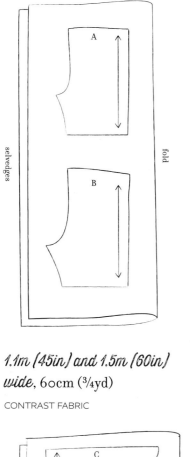

1.1m (45in) and 1.5m (60in) wide, 60cm (³⁄₄yd)

CONTRAST FABRIC

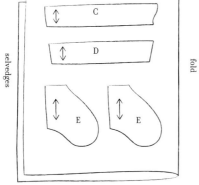

Full-length version

1.1m (45in) and 1.5m (60in) wide, 2.4m (2⁵⁄₈yd)

MAIN FABRIC

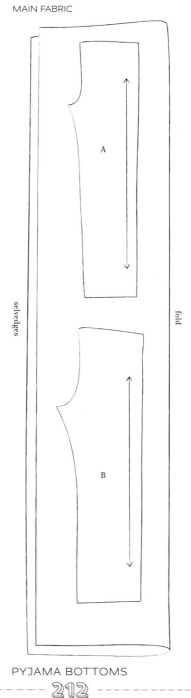

A – front leg
B – back leg
C – front hem facing
D – back hem facing
E – pocket bag

YOKE TOP

1.1m (45in) and 1.5m (60in) wide

For the collar, fold fabric at 45° to the selvedge, you will need approx 60cm (24¾in) for this.

A – front bodice
B – back bodice
C – front yoke
D – back yoke
E – collar

1.1m (45in) and 1.5m (60in) wide, 60cm (23 ¾in)

COLLAR FABRIC

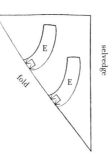

1.1m (45in), 1.9m (2yd)

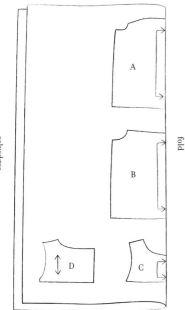

1.5m (60in) wide, 1.5m (1⅝yd)

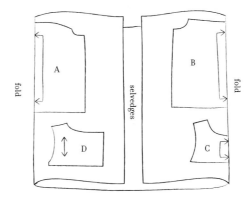

PICK YOUR POCKETS SKIRT

For the variation: replace front pocket pieces E & F with side seam pocket piece G (so that you have four of pocket piece G when everything is cut out)

A – skirt front
B – skirt back
C – front yoke
D – back yoke
E – front pocket bag
F – front pocket bearer
G – side seam pocket bag

1.1m (45in) wide, 1.5m (1⅝yd)

MAIN FABRIC (IF YOU ARE USING A CONTRAST FABRIC FOR YOUR POCKETS, THEN YOU WILL NEED SLIGHTLY LESS MAIN FABRIC, AND DON'T FORGET TO CUT OUT YOUR POCKET PIECES FROM THE CONTRAST FABRIC)

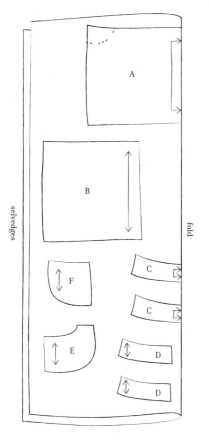

1.5m (60in) wide, 1.3m (1½yd)

MAIN FABRIC (IF YOU ARE USING A CONTRAST FABRIC FOR YOUR POCKETS, THEN YOU WILL NEED SLIGHTLY LESS MAIN FABRIC, AND DON'T FORGET TO CUT OUT YOUR POCKET PIECES FROM THE CONTRAST FABRIC)

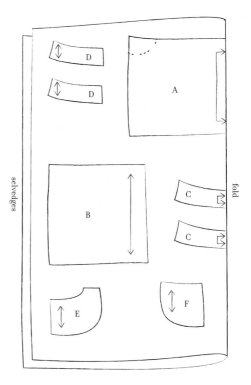

HAVE IT YOUR WAY DRESS

For the variation: replace curved collar
piece E with pointed collar piece F, and
curved sleeve pieces I & J for puff sleeve
pieces K & L. If you want a contrast collar
(as in the main version on page 200) then
you will need some contrast fabric too

A – front bodice
B – back bodice
C – skirt front
D – skirt back
E – curved collar
F – pointed collar
G – front facing
H – back facing
I – curved sleeve facing
J – curved sleeve
K – puff sleeve
L – puff sleeve cuff

1.1m (45in) wide, 2.7m (3yd) for both the
curved and puff sleeve options

MAIN FABRIC

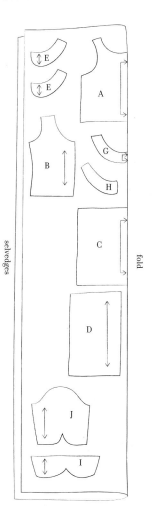

1.5m (60in) wide, 2m (2¼yd) for both the
curved and the puff sleeve variations

MAIN FABRIC

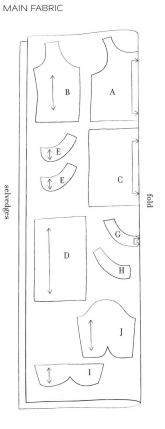

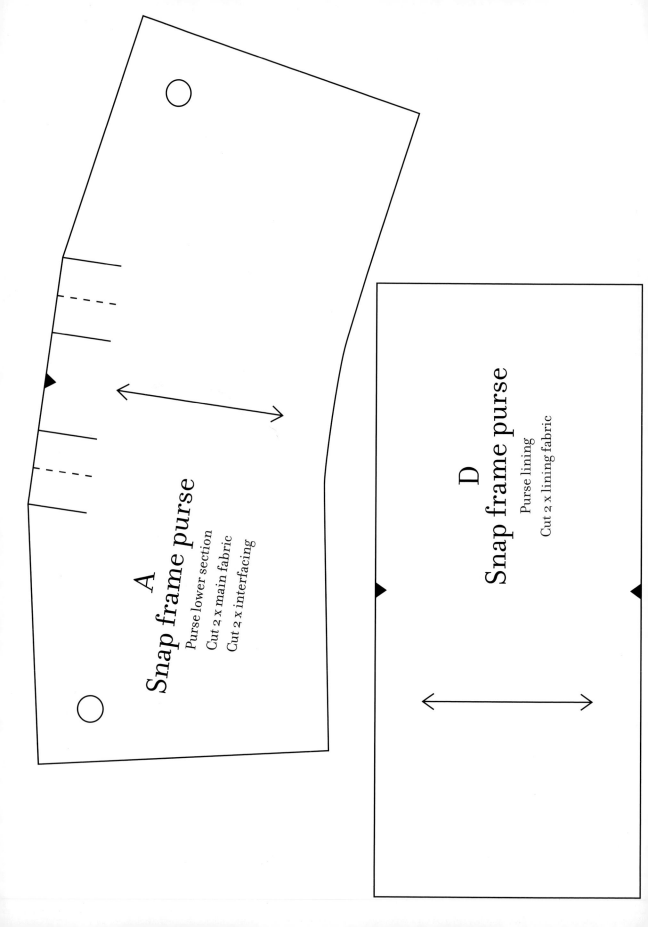

A
Snap frame purse

Purse lower section

Cut 2 x main fabric
Cut 2 x interfacing

D
Snap frame purse

Purse lining
Cut 2 x lining fabric

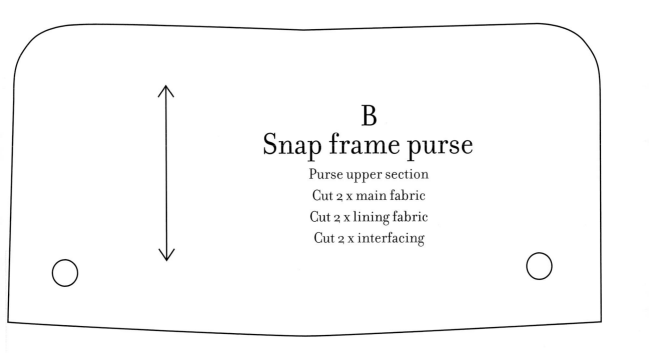

B
Snap frame purse

Purse upper section

Cut 2 x main fabric

Cut 2 x lining fabric

Cut 2 x interfacing

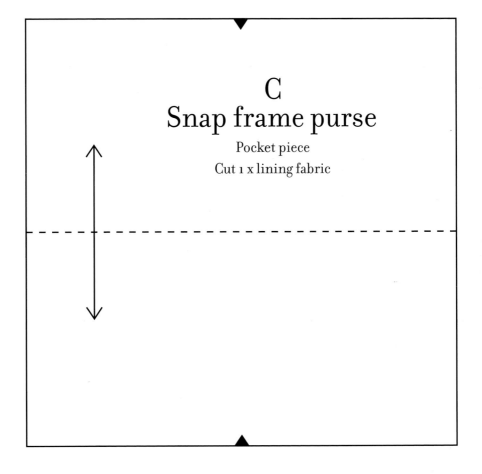

C
Snap frame purse

Pocket piece

Cut 1 x lining fabric

Glossary

backstitch A strong hand-sewing stitch in which the needle is brought up ahead of the previous stitch and taken down at the end of it, forming an unbroken line. On the wrong side the stitches overlap. A few individual backstitches are often worked on top of each other to fasten a thread.

bar tack A set of stitches used to reinforce an opening, such as a fly front, or the ends of a buttonhole. It can be worked by hand or by machine, using a close zigzag stitch.

bias In fabric, the direction forming an angle, especially a 45-degree angle (sometimes called the 'true bias'), to the *warp* and *weft* threads; the direction in which the fabric can easily be stretched. See also *grain*.

bias binding A strip of fabric cut on the *bias* and typically used for edging garments, commonly at the neckline or armhole. Also used in making *piping*.

blind hem A method of hemming whereby the stitching is not visible from the right side/outside of the garment. It can be worked by hand or by machine, using a blind hem foot.

casing A channel for encasing elastic or cord created either by folding the fabric over itself and sewing it in place or by sewing on a strip of bias binding, ribbon or other material.

catch stitch (also called 'herringbone stitch') A hand-sewing stitch, commonly used for hemming, which produces small diagonal crosses. Only a few threads of the outer fabric are caught, so that the stitching is virtually invisible from the right side.

facing A section of fabric attached to the inside of a garment, often at the neckline or around the armhole, which helps to hold the shape of the garment, while enclosing the raw edges.

fat quarter A piece of fabric formed by cutting a metre (or a yard), then cutting it in half crossways and then lengthways. The term derives from American fabrics, which are measured by the yard; a 'fat quarter' (of a yard) is a more versatile amount, for patchwork, than a normal quarter of a yard, which measures 23cm (9in) across the width of the fabric.

feed dogs The notched piece of metal under the needle plate of a sewing machine that moves the fabric backwards or forwards, as required, under the machine foot as you sew.

grain This refers to the direction of the threads that are woven to make up the fabric; the lengthways grain, or *warp*, runs parallel to the *selvedge*; the crossways grain, or *weft*, runs at a 90-degree angle to it.

grain line A line marked on a pattern piece that should be positioned on the fabric's lengthways *grain*, parallel to the selvedge, in order for that section to hang correctly.

gusset A piece of fabric inserted in a garment or accessory to create depth or provide extra width.

hand-tack To join two or more layers temporarily using large *running stitches*, about 1–2cm (⅜–¾in) long, before joining them permanently, usually by machine. Also called simply 'tack'.

ladder stitch A hand-sewing stitch, typically used to join two folds of fabric neatly and unobtrusively. The tiny stitches across the folded edges resemble the rungs of a ladder.

machine-tack To join two or more layers temporarily by machine, using a long stitch length so that the stitches can easily be removed later.

piping A length of cord covered with bias binding. It can be made in different thicknesses depending on the diameter of the cord.

running stitch The simplest of all hand stitches; it consists of passing the needle alternately up and down through the fabric in one direction. The stitches can vary in length depending on the function of the stitch. It can be used decoratively, as in quilting, or to *hand-tack* two or more layers of fabric together, or sometimes to gather an edge.

seam allowance The distance between the line of stitching in a seam and the raw edge of the fabric. It can vary in width depending on the project, but most commonly is 1.5cm (⅝in).

selvedge The firm, non-fraying edges of a woven fabric, formed by the *weft* threads doubling back on themselves through the *warp*.

sleeve head The top section of a sleeve, which fits into the bodice or main body of a garment.

stay stitching Straight machine stitching, used to prevent curved sections of fabric from stretching or distorting out of shape. It is commonly used around necklines and is sewn at the edge of the fabric within the seam allowance.

tailor's tack A method used to transfer pattern markings onto fabric using a needle and thread, leaving long tail threads. Once the markings are no longer required, they can quickly and easily be removed.

topstitching Machine stitching that is sewn on the right side of the fabric, usually close to an edge or seamline, often as a decorative feature.

understitching Similar to topstitching, but sewn on the inside of a garment or accessory, commonly on a facing, near the seamline joining it to the main piece; the stitching helps to hold the facing and the seam allowances on the inside, so that they don't roll outwards.

walking foot A special machine foot that has *feed dogs* on the underside; these enable the upper layer(s) of fabric to move at the same rate as the one underneath and so avoid slipping out of alignment. It is especially useful when stitching thicker fabrics or multiple layers of fabric together.

warp The threads in a woven fabric that run parallel to the selvedge; also known as the lengthways *grain*.

weft The threads in a woven fabric that run at a 90-degree angle to the selvedge; also known as the crossways *grain*.

Inspiration

Here are some of my favourite places to look for tips, techniques, ideas and inspiration.

www.sewmamasew.com www.makeitcoats.com
www.tillyandthebuttons.com www.pinterest.com
www.coletterie.com www.blogforbettersewing.com

FURTHER READING

The Colette Sewing Handbook by Sarai Mitnick

Dressmaking by Alison Smith

Embroidered Effects: Projects and Patterns to Inspire Your Stitching (Sublime Stitching) by Jenny Hart

Me and My Sewing Machine by Kate Haxell

Embroidery Stitch Bible by Betty Barnden

USEFUL ADDRESSES

Fabric and supplies

Guthrie & Ghani
169, Alcester Road
Moseley
Birmingham
B13 8JR
www.guthrie-ghani.co.uk

The Eternal Maker
41, Terminus Road
Chichester
West Sussex
PO19 8TX
www.eternalmaker.com

Misan Textiles
4 Berwick Street
London
W1F 0DR
www.misan.co.uk

Liberty London
Regent Street
London
W1B 5AH
www.liberty.co.uk

Emma Hardicker
www.emmahardicker.com

The Cloth House
47 and 98 Berwick Street
London
W1F 8SJ
www.clothhouse.com

Mandors Fabric Store
134 Renfrew St
Glasgow
G3 6ST
131, East Claremont St
Edinburgh
EH7 4JA
www.mandors.co.uk

Fabrics Galore
52-54 Lavender Hill
London
SW11 5RH
www.fabricsgalore.co.uk

Ray-stitch
99 Essex Road
London
N1 2SJ
www.raystitch.co.uk

Index

Acknowledgements

Writing this book has been one of the most exciting opportunities I've ever had. I love to share my passion for sewing and being creative so having my own book with which to do that feels awesome! It's not until you start the process of a project like this that you realize how many people trust, help and support you, so it's hard to know where to begin – so many people have played a part in getting me through it all.

There are the new people whom I've met along the way who have given me such great opportunities: the team at Love Productions for selecting me to be part of the first series of *The Great British Sewing Bee;* Stuart at Metrostar for taking me on, believing in my ideas and helping me put my proposals together; Denise Bates for also believing in me and my ideas, and for trusting that I could write this book; the lovely bunch of talented people who have made this book look so great including Pauline, Miranda, Grace, Eleanor and, of course, Nassima with her amazing photography skills; I'm sure there are more of you and I'm so grateful for all the work you have done! And a huge thank you to Eileen Simmons and Sharon at South & City College, Birmingham, for taking so much of their own time to help draft my designs and grade the patterns for me.

Then there are all my family and friends, you might not know it but I couldn't have done anything that I have without you. Thank you to my mum, Fiona, for being such a great role model and inspiration, and for teaching me to sew in the first place. Also, thank you to Mum, and my dad, Gordon, for always being there, listening, giving me advice and proofreading text for me. My amazing husband Ayaz, who has had to put up with me stressing out and working *all* the time – you are my rock! My good friends and colleagues Lucy, Sarah and Vanessa who have kept me sane and my business running while I worked hard on the book. Thank you to my *Sewing Bee* friends Tilly, Stuart and Sandra for all the chats and advice and just generally knowing what it's like when no one else does. And, finally, thank you to all my other friends and family for just being such an amazing bunch of people to know!